JUL - - 2005

Holocaust Heroes and Nazi Criminals

Anne Frank

Hope in the Shadows of the Holocaust

Spring Hermann

Enslow Publishers, Inc.

40 Industrial Road	PO Box 38
Box 398	Aldershot
Berkeley Heights, NJ 07922	Hants GU12 6BP
USA	UK

http://www.enslow.com

For Margo and Jessica—love always.
And for the cast, crew, and directors of The Diary of Anne Frank, produced by
Belleville Township High School, 1960. Slowly but surely we learned.

Acknowledgements

The Greater Hartford Jewish Community Center
Koopman Library, and Beatrice Brodie, librarian.

Library of Congress Cataloging-in-Publication Data:

Hermann, Spring.
   Anne Frank : hope in the shadows of the Holocaust /
   Spring Hermann.—1st ed.
      p. cm. — (Holocaust heroes and Nazi criminals)
   Includes bibliographical references and index.
   ISBN 0-7660-2531-4
      1. Frank, Anne, 1929–1945—Juvenile literature. 2. Jews—Netherlands—Amsterdam—
Biography—Juvenile literature. 3. Holocaust, Jewish (1939–1945)—Netherlands—
Amsterdam—Biography—Juvenile literature.
   4. Jewish children in the Holocaust—Netherlands—Amsterdam—Biography—
Juvenile literature. 5. Amsterdam (Netherlands)—Biography—Juvenile literature.
   I. Title. II. Series.
   DS135.N6F73344 2004
   940.53′18′092—dc22

                                                2004016154

Printed in the United States of America

10 9 8 7 6 5 4 3 2 1

To Our Readers: We have done our best to make sure all Internet Addresses in this book were active and appropriate when we went to press. However, the author and the publisher have no control over and assume no liability for the material available on those Internet sites or on other Web sites they may link to. Any comments or suggestions can be sent by e-mail to comments@enslow.com or to the address on the back cover.

Illustration Credits: 1960 *Bellevinois*, p. 132; Corbis, pp. 70, 92; Enslow Publishers, Inc., p. 5; Getty Images, pp. 3, 4, 6, 7, 11, 15, 20, 24, 35, 48, 72, 83, 121, 134 (top), 138, 154, 156, 158; Hadassah Bimko Rosensaft, courtesy of USHMM, p. 119; Harry Lore, courtesy of the USHMM photo archives, p. 137 (top); National Archives and Records Administration, pp. 33, 46, 88, 96, 134 (third from top); Spring Hermann, pp. 58, 67, 78, 99; USHMM, pp. 22, 134 (second from bottom), 135 (top), 137 (second from bottom); USHMM, courtesy of the Israel Government Press Office, p. 54; USHMM, courtesy of KZ Gedenkstatte Dachau, p. 116; USHMM, courtesy of Lorenz Schmuhl, pp. 108, 134 (third from bottom), 136 (top), 137 (third from bottom); USHMM, courtesy of the Main Commission for the Persecution of the Crimes Against the Polish Nation, pp. 134 (second from top), 136 (bottom), 137 (second from top); USHMM, courtesy of the National Museum of American Jewish History, pp. 134 (bottom), 135 (bottom), 137 (bottom).

Cover Illustration: Getty Images; USHMM, courtesy of Lorenz Schmuhl (background).

Contents

Fast Facts About Anne Frank

Full Name: Annelies Marie Frank

Birth Date: June 12, 1929

Birth Place: Frankfurt, Germany

Family: Mother, Edith Hollander; father, Otto Frank; sister, Margot Betti Frank; grandmother, Alice Stern Frank; grandmother, Rosa Hollander

First Home: A duplex townhouse at 307 Marbachweg in Frankfurt, Germany

Immigration: Moved to Amsterdam in February 1934

Languages: German, Dutch, some English

Schools Attended: Montessori School, 1934–1941; Jewish Lyceum (1941–1942)

Into Hiding: Anne and her family went into hiding in a secret annex on July 5, 1942

Annex Occupants: Anne, Edith, Otto and Margot Frank; Hermann, Gusti, and Peter van Pels; and Dr. Fritz Pfeffer

Those Who Helped Anne: Miep and Jan Gies, Bep Voskuijl, Victor Kugler, Johannes Kleiman

Journal Name: Anne called her journal "Kitty"

Caught: Anne and her family were discovered and arrested on August 4, 1944

Concentration Camp Incarcerations: Westerbork (August 1944); Auschwitz (August–October 1944); Bergen-Belsen (October 1944–March 1945)

Death: March 1945 at Bergen-Belsen concentration camp from malnutrition and typhus

North Sea

Baltic Sea

**Westerbork Camp
(August 1944)**

**Bergen-Belsen Camp
(October 1944 until her
death in March 1945)**

NETHERLANDS

③

⑤

POLAND

②

**Amsterdam
(1934–August 1944)**

Berlin

**Auschwitz Camp
(August 1944–
October 1944)**

BELGIUM

• Leipzig

**Frankfurt
(1929–1934)**

①

④

CZECH REPUBLIC

FRANCE

• Stuttgart

GERMANY

AUSTRIA

SWITZERLAND

This map shows Anne's journey through Europe during her short life.

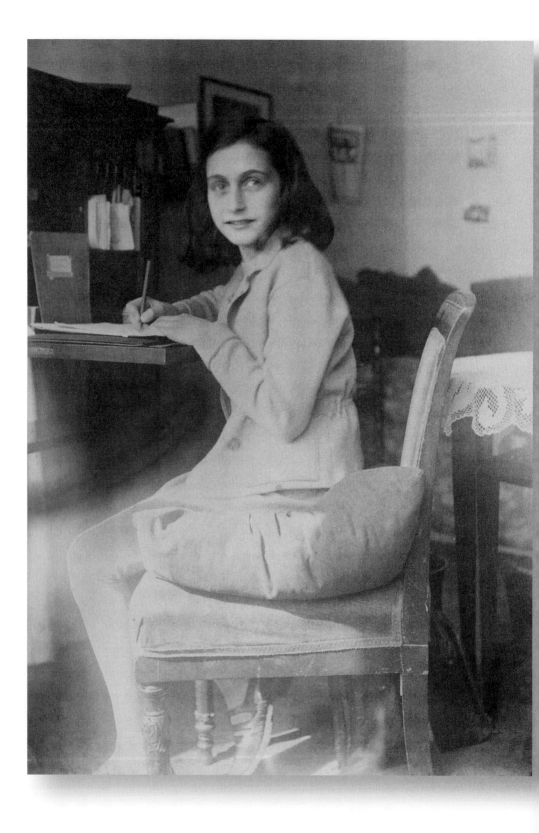

1

Anne Frank Enters a Changing World

Annelies Marie Frank took her first look at the world on June 12, 1929, in the old German city of Frankfurt am Main [on the Main River], in a maternity hospital.[1] Anne, as she was always to be called, nestled in her mother Edith Hollander-Frank's arms. She was immediately adored by her father Otto. Anne's older sister Margot Betti, born in February 1926, had to wait until Edith's mother Rosa Hollander brought her for a visit. Reportedly, Margot was tickled to see her baby sister, who had thick spiky black hair. Edith recorded in Margot's baby book that upon seeing the baby, "Margot is completely delighted."[2] Anne spent twelve days in the clinic with her mother. Long maternity ward stays were common then, and Edith had had a difficult labor.

For a colicky infant who had breathing problems, Anne was a strong willed, 8½ pound baby with a loud cry. The Franks lived in an apartment in the outskirts of Frankfurt, a city that had been home to Otto's family since the seventeenth century.[3] At the beginning of their marriage, Anne's parents lived with Grandmother Alice Frank in the city's prosperous Westend. It was customary for European couples to return to a family home after marriage. If the home was large enough, they raised their children there. Although Anne's grandmother's home was spacious, Edith wanted a different atmosphere for her children. Frankfurt was a busy city in 1929, with over 540,000 residents and many run-down inner city areas.[4] Edith urged Otto to move out to the suburbs. She wanted Margot and Anne to play in their own small garden and breathe fresh air.

Anne's first home at 307 Marbachweg was a stucco duplex townhouse in which the Franks occupied the first two floors of the right half. Waiting to help Edith with this demanding baby was Kathi Stilgenbauer, their housekeeper. Grandmother Rosa Hollander visited to help out as well.[5] Kathi had a small bedroom on the second floor, as did Margot. Grandmother Alice Frank also came to admire her new granddaughter. This close family enveloped Anne with love and attention. She was taken in a stroller for many outings in Frankfurt's summer sun, unaware of the turbulent times around her.

Germany Reels from WWI Losses

In the 1920s, Anne's native country was deeply troubled. Nearly ten million Europeans died fighting in World War I, with over thirty million wounded or imprisoned. Germany was defeated; much of its male population had been killed or injured. Political instability and economic chaos ensued in the German Republic. The Treaty of Versailles, signed in 1919, punished the German government by forcing it to pay huge "reparations" or monies to the victorious allied nations to cover all their war damages.

In Article 231 of the treaty, Germany was made completely responsible for the war. The German people had to pay over $32 billion over a 40-year period. Great Britain and France, both of whom had taken loans from the United States to wage the war, wanted their shares of the reparations as soon as possible. The Germans were forced to give up their weapons and most of their armies and merchant fleet. With the *mark* (German currency) having so little to back it up in goods, the prospect of paying out billions of dollars seemed impossible for the Germans to contemplate.

The German people were upset. They had taken no territory during the war. No outside forces were occupying their lands. They had agreed to make a peace settlement. According to historian Eleanor L. Turk, they felt "the Allies had turned an honorable truce into a disastrous defeat for Germany."[6] Postwar unemployment and chaos in Germany's financial institutions made recovery even more difficult. A large percentage of the surviving soldiers from World War I returned to Germany to find no jobs and their families on hard times.

National Socialists Start to Rise

A radical socialist group called the National Socialist German Worker's Party (NSDAP), claimed to be Germany's defense against left-wing communist parties, and played on the Germans' wounded sense of national pride. The initials of this party, founded in 1920, came from part of the German spelling of the party: **NA**tional so**ZI**alistiche (National Socialist), or NAZI. Its elected leader was a young, ambitious, racist politician named Adolf Hitler.[7]

When they organized in the 1920s, the Nazi party leaders wrote a twenty-five-point program. In Point 4, the plan stated: "Only members of the nation may be citizens of the

State. Only those of German blood, whatever their creed, may be members of the nation. Accordingly no Jew may be a member of the nation."[8]

More Economic Disaster

In October 1929, the New York stock market, the most influential in the world, suffered its worst panic selloff in history. In what was termed "The Crash," or "Black Thursday," millions of ordinary people lost their life savings, and by the end of October 24, 1929, eleven major financiers on Wall Street had committed suicide.[9] Banks around the world closed.

Because Otto's father Michael had been the president of a small international banking firm, the crash affected the Frank family severely. Although he had started out in other businesses, Otto Frank worked in the family institution. By 1925, the family was in debt. Otto had failed to find a love match and was lonely. He longed to have children before he was too old. He also wanted a wife with a dowry that would help keep his business afloat. Through family introductions, Otto won the hand of Edith Hollander, from Aachem. It was obvious that Edith's generous dowry cleared up the Frank family debts.[10] They married on Otto's thirty-sixth birthday, on May 12, 1925, when Edith was twenty-five years old.

Religious Differences between Edith and Otto

Anne Frank's comfortable middle class family was Jewish. Edith had insisted on a Jewish marriage and continued celebrating her religious holidays in the home and in the synagogue. Edith's family had been Orthodox and kept a kosher kitchen. "Keeping kosher" meant observing the strict Jewish dietary laws about the slaughtering, harvesting, preparing, and serving of food. Edith compromised with her

Otto Heinrich Frank

Born in Frankfurt, Germany, in May 1889, Otto's successful family owned a banking concern, and a medicinal throat lozenge company. Slender, handsome and bright, Otto, after graduating from a Gymnasium, went to the University of Heidelberg. There he met an American Jew and fellow student, Nathan Straus, whose father was half-owner of Macy's department store in New York.[11] After only one semester at the University, Otto took an internship at Macy's to study American business culture in 1909. He returned home in 1910, then worked in business in Dusseldorf, until he was called up for the military in 1915.[12]

Otto fought with the German infantry in World War I. Lieutenant Otto Frank was awarded the Iron Cross for bravery.[13] When the war ended in 1918 with a German defeat, Otto went back to help his widowed mother run their troubled bank. In 1923, Otto opened a branch of the Frank bank in Amsterdam, a city that he would later adopt as his own. His marriage to Edith Hollander from Aachem was arranged through family introductions, a way that was common in Europe. He was devoted to Edith, and the two daughters they had, for the rest of their lives together.

husband and became a Reform Jew; Reform Jews are not as strict as Orthodox Jews. In her tiny home office, she used her desk to manage her family accounts, and kept her Hebrew prayer books on her bookshelf. Otto came from a liberal Jewish family and had little religious education. He and his brothers did not receive a *bar mitzvah*, the religious rite that trains Jewish boys to read the scriptures in Hebrew, and receives them into the faith at age thirteen. After they moved to Marbachweg, Edith Frank joined the Westend synagogue near Otto's family home, and traveled back there often for religious observances.[14]

The history of persecution and tolerance for Germany's Jews swung back and forth through the centuries. From the Middle Ages through the eighteenth century, Jews in Frankfurt had been forced to live in their own neighborhood, a walled ghetto. Often through the years they had to observe an evening curfew. Institutions were openly anti-Semitic, meaning they held ill feelings toward the Jews.

By 1800, this forced segregation ended. The Anne Frank Foundation scholars state: "Jews were given equal rights under the law, setting in motion a process of social and cultural assimilation."[15] By 1929, about 5.5 percent of Frankfurt's population, or about thirty thousand residents, were Jewish. Otto Frank's family openly prospered in the banking business, while strongly identifying themselves as German citizens.

In countries in Eastern Europe such as Russia and Poland, the nineteenth century became a dangerous time for Jews. Pogroms, or organized persecution of Jews, forced many thousands to pack up what little they could carry and head for more tolerant countries. Although some immigrated to the United States, many other Polish Jews fled to what they thought was the safer political climate of Germany. In Germany in 1848, Jews joined Christians in uprising against the oppressive Frederick Wilhelm IV, rebelling for constitutional freedom. A German rabbi wrote at this time: "We are and only wish to be Germans! . . . We are no longer Israelites in anything but our beliefs—in every other aspect we very much belong to the state in which we live."[16]

Jews Become Scapegoats for Germany's Problems

Otto Frank and his brothers Herbert and Robert had joined at least one hundred thousand Jews who fought in the German army in World War I, risking their lives for their country.[17] Most banks, including those that were controlled by Jews, loaned the government whatever they needed to support the war. When Germany surrendered, Jewish businessmen were among those who bore the burden of the defeat and economic collapse, including the Frank family. Yet the Jews gradually became the target of national frustration. When economic conditions grew harsh in post-World War I Germany, and political activists became extreme, the times were ripe for finding a group to blame. Jews were a unified successful and religious group, who could be easily identified.

The German economy in general had picked up in the late 1920s, due to some $200 million in loans from American banks. However, by the end of 1929, overall financial problems from the stock market crash were severely affecting the Frank's bank and throat lozenge business. Soon Otto had to move both businesses into a small, shared building to save money.

Anne's First Years

Hostility and anti-Semitism had not yet affected the average German Jewish family. Edith and Otto kept their little girls cozy and safe. Delight in their daughters Margot and Anne always lifted their spirits. In an interview in 1954, Otto stated that he liked to care for the girls each evening, although with baby Anne, the care stretched far into the night. Anne was restless and slept poorly, so often Otto found himself "going in to her many times, petting her and singing nursery songs to quieten her."[18] After a lot of painful digestive problems, Anne started to thrive. Margot was a more tranquil child who related strongly to her mother.

Anne's neighborhood enjoyed a mix of families from all religions. Next door to the Franks at 305 Marbachweg lived the landlord of the duplex, Protestant Otto Konitzer with his wife and three children. In the flat above them lived the Catholic Staub family, with two young daughters. In the next house, the Naumann family, also Catholic, was raising six children. Little Margot Frank was easily accepted into the gang of children. The youngest of the Naumann children, Gertrud, was devoted to Margot and Anne. As she became an adolescent, she often babysat for them. When the Catholic Staub and Naumann children played an indoor game of "church," they coached little Margot in playing altar boy.

At the end of 1929, the Frank's housekeeper Kathi Stilgenbauer left to get married. Otto must have had mixed feelings about losing Kathi, whom Edith and the children loved, because keeping a servant was an expense they could not afford. Before she left, Kathi asked Otto what he thought about

In her diary, Anne captioned this photo "Papa with his two sprogs." It shows Otto and his children, Margot and Anne, in 1930.

the "Brown Shirts." These men were the brown-uniformed militia of the Nazi party, termed *Sturmabteilung* (Storm Troopers). They had started to march through neighborhoods with Jewish populations, harassing and threatening, breaking into shops and homes.[19] Kathi recalled that Otto tried to "make a joke of the whole thing . . . But Mrs. Frank looked up from her plate and she fixed her eyes on us and said, 'We'll find out soon enough who they are, Kathi.'"[20]

Depression Fuels German Socialists

By Anne's first birthday in June 1930, the financial depression set off by the stock market crash now seemed to affect all world markets. The German economy, due to war losses and enormous unemployment, was struggling. The Nazis began hinting to the German public, if only pure-blooded Germans were in charge of all German businesses and institutions, if only the Jews and communists and Gypsies could be controlled, Germany would rise again. Amazingly, more and more people, especially the poor and unemployed, started listening to them.

In the first Reichstag (legislative) election in September 1930, the Nazi candidates got 18 percent of the vote, a respectable count for a small socialist party. Their appeal was rising dramatically.[21] Otto Frank read in a 1925 Nazi book called *Mein Kampf* that its author Adolf Hitler, in his vision for reshaping Germany, actually advocated that the government during World War I should have "exterminated the Jews mercilessly."[22] Patriotic Otto must have been stunned by such an outrageous theory. That year, Otto's cousin Milly Stanfield who lived in England came to visit. She remembered Otto saying that he did not know what was going to happen to Germany. The power of the super nationalist

Nazis scared him. He saw something evil coming at a time when not too many other Jews were taking it seriously.

The Franks Move to the "Poet's Corner"

By the winter of 1931, relations between the Franks and their landlord Mr. Konitzer deteriorated. Although the Franks were a model family who paid their rent, Konitzer was uncomfortable housing a devout Jew like Edith Frank. He was openly sympathetic to the Nazi party, saluting the Brown Shirts as they marched. Although Otto later claimed he moved his family because he needed to find cheaper housing, their good neighbors the Naumanns and the Staubs disagreed. Historian Melissa Muller stated the Naumanns told her the Franks moved "because they could no longer stand the malicious atmosphere in their landlord's house."[23]

Edith and Otto moved into their smaller but pleasant apartment on #24 Ganghoferstrasse, in a neighborhood called Poet's Corner. Anne stayed with the Naumanns during the move. The family settled into a middle class neighborhood, which although more urban, was still free of harassment by the Nazi Storm Troopers.

Jews joined in cooperative groups, such as the Committee of the Israelite Community. By 1932, industrial activity was down 65 percent and over seventy thousand of Frankfurt's population was unemployed, with a full 25 percent of its workers no longer having steady income.[24] The Jews realized that if they did not band together to help each other, they could be ruined. They offered each other financial and personal support.

Anne Holds the Center of Attention

June 1932 was a happy time for Anne, now a lively three-year-old. She played in her garden sandbox with toys or

17

played games on her child-sized set of garden furniture. Edith took Anne on outings down the treed paths through her neighborhood, while six-year-old Margot was off in school.[25] Margot attended a progressive school with children of all backgrounds. Often Gertrud and the Naumann and Staub children came over to play with Margot and Anne. As the baby in the family, Anne soon learned how to keep up with her older sister's friends. With huge dark eyes, impish smile, and delightful verbal skills, she usually got the attention she wanted. If that failed, she tried a piercing wail that usually moved Otto's heart.

During the summer, Otto told his mother that financially, there was "no way forward . . . I always tried to sweep problems under the carpet but that's no longer viable . . . " He then added that Margot was always an angel, "she had a school outing today. She was thrilled."[26] Otto wrote to his sister Leni Elias who lived in Basel that although business was certainly bad, the bright spot in his life was the children, who always took his mind off his troubles.

In other parts of Frankfurt in 1932, young girls were being inducted into a different way of life. The Nazis had begun a youth organization called the *Bund Deutscher Madel*, or League of German Girls. At first the League seemed like a girls' sports club, teaching discipline, duty, and healthy living. Since Germans had long loved athletic clubs, the League grew popular. Gradually, girls in the League were taught something darker by their leaders: Avoid all contact with Jewish girls.

During the summer of 1932, the Nazi party won 37 percent of the votes and doubled its seats in the Reichstag.[27] This was not yet the majority of voters, but made the Nazis the strongest of the political parties.

The Franks Move Back to Grandmother's House

Otto's mother Alice offered her home to his family again. He convinced Edith they could not afford to pass up the chance to live rent-free. The family moved back to Alice Frank's home on Mertonstrasse in March 1933. Before they left their old neighborhood, Otto had heard the Brown Shirts marching and singing a song with the line: "When Jewish blood splatters off the knife."[28] The Poet's Corner was no longer safe. This made the future to Otto all too clear.

Edith and Otto knew their move back to Alice Frank's home could only be temporary. What they had to start contemplating was a move out of their beloved homeland. At the rate the Nazi party was taking over, in a few years the German government would turn against all Jews. They had to determine when to leave and where to go to allow Otto to make a living.

2

From Frankfurt to Amsterdam

Living with Grandmother Frank apparently gave Otto and Edith enough spare income to enjoy some of life's little pleasures. Edith and her girls shopped in Frankfurt's city center, where they could visit museums, cafes and ice cream parlors.[1] In the winter of 1933, Anne at age four was an active youngster, compared to the neat, reserved Margot. Their former housekeeper Kathi Stilgenbauer remembered that Anne often toddled into trouble, happily sitting in rain puddles and needing to have her clothes changed several times a day. Margot, however, was amazingly clean and could wear outfits for many days: "It was as though dirt did not exist for her . . . dirt simply did not touch her."[2]

As Edith, Anne, and Margot traveled around the city that first winter of Nazi rule in 1933, they could not avoid troops of uniformed soldiers. These men carried enormous red, white, and black flags, bearing the Nazi swastika emblem.

Demonstrations on the steps of Town Hall featured soldiers saluting Adolf Hitler and screaming *"Juden raus! Juden raus!"*[3] While the anti-Semitic chants of *Jews Out* continued, bystanders joined in. Historian Carol Ann Lee wrote about the appearance of a "new form of graffiti: damning anti-Semitic slogans daubed in white paint across Jewish-owned shop windows."[4]

Repressive Laws Curb Jewish Freedom

One of the Nazis' first anti-Jewish laws to be passed stated that Jewish children could not attend the schools of their choice. This deeply upset Otto and Edith Frank. They had enrolled Anne in a nursery school for the fall of 1933, which would now be forbidden to her. Margot would be forced to leave the school in which she was thriving. She was enrolled in a public school near Grandmother Frank's house, where she sat in a rear corner with the few other Jewish children. The Franks, for whom freedom of education was important, decided that their days in Germany were ending.

Otto investigated Switzerland (home of his sister Leni); England (where his brother Robert and cousin Milli lived); America (where other relatives were heading); and the Netherlands, a country with a long reputation of being tolerant of all religions. Otto had already done banking business in the Netherlands. Given its policy of neutrality, and its population of over one hundred thousand Jews, Otto felt this nation would protect them.

During the month of April 1933, anti-Jewish legislation continued to be rammed through the Reichstag. On April 7, the "Reform of the Civil Service Law" decreed "all institutions of the Reich, . . . including schools and universities, were to be 'cleansed.'"[5] Jews in Civil Service lost their jobs.

Young Adolf Hitler

Adolf Hitler was born April 20, 1889, in Austria, to Alois Schicklgruber Hitler, and Klara Poelzl Hitler.[6] Historian Ian Kershaw said Alois was described as "overbearing, a stern, distant, often irritable father."[7] Adolf and his little sister Paula received their only affection from their hard-working mother. Alois frequently beat Adolf.

Adolf dropped out of school to prepare himself to become an artist. When he applied to the Vienna Academy of Fine Arts, he was rejected both times. Her husband having already died, Klara Hitler died of cancer in 1907. Hitler described later in his book *Mein Kampf* ("My Struggle") that her death was "a dreadful blow . . . my mother I had loved."[8]

The Aryan race, who the ancient Greeks claimed came from Thule [modern day Iceland and Norway], became one of Hitler's obsessions. He picked up his political education from certain Viennese politicians, who taught that the Jew was the cause of "all chaos, corruption, and destruction" in culture and economy.[9]

After a move to Munich, Hitler joined the German Army in World War I. When Germany lost, Adolf was very upset. In *Mein Kampf*, he warned against growing domination by the Jews.[10] By age thirty, Hitler believed he was destined to lead Germany back to world power. It would take his fledgling socialist/nationalist party over a decade to gain control.

All Jews, and those who opposed the policies of the Nazi party, were seen as enemies.

During May 1933, Nazi agitators organized book burnings in major German cities. Otto Frank watched the works of admired writers Heinrich Mann, Thomas Mann, Bertolt Brecht, Erich Maria Remarque, and poet Heinrich Heine, and many others go up in flames because the authors were either Jews, homosexuals, or too close to communism in their philosophy.[11] However, other books were being highly praised, such as a sort of textbook which appeared in classrooms. *The Poisonous Mushroom* taught children that "just as a single poisonous mushroom can kill a whole family, so a solitary Jew can destroy a whole village, a whole city, a whole people."[12]

A Nazi officer named Heinrich Himmler, then Police President of Munich, quietly put into motion a plan for jailing political enemies of the Nazis. He turned a gunpowder factory in the town of Dachau, north of Munich, into a barbed-wire "concentration camp." Those jailed in the Dachau camp would perform slave labor in armament factories.[13] Police forces of German cities were infiltrated by the Nazi elite corps. Scholar Richard Rhodes explained that the SS (*Schutzstaffel*) which meant "defense echelon," was a police force that answered directly to Hitler, outside constraints of German law.[14] Thousands of these SS officers would be running German law enforcement, with Heinrich Himmler as their top man.

Otto Frank Plans the Family's Exodus

Otto appealed to his sister's husband Erich Elias, who was the Swiss branch manager of an international company called Opetka. The two men worked out a deal where Otto became the manager of the Dutch branch of this company in

Amsterdam. He found himself in the business of selling pectin, a product that is needed to make jams and jellies. Otto took a room in Amsterdam, where he began setting up offices, looking for a staff, and seeking a new apartment for his family.

Before they left Frankfurt, the Frank family returned to their old neighborhood to see the Naumann family. Gertrud Naumann recalled the poignant visit: "Mr. Frank never spoke about anything that troubled him. But . . . you could see the way it was worrying him."[15] As they finished their coffee, Anne, having just turned four, frowned seriously at Mr. Naumann and remarked: "Why, you have eyes like a cat."[16] Although Anne's parents were embarrassed, everyone laughed. It was unlikely the families would ever be neighbors again.

Partly for emotional comfort and partly to save money, Edith took Anne and Margot to spend the fall in Aachem, Germany, near the Dutch border, with her widowed mother. Grandma (*Oma* in German) Hollander and Anne adored each other. Oma was sweet and patient with active, talkative and temperamental children. Anne often went for walks or streetcar rides with Oma. Once they rode the crowded streetcar home, and Anne loudly piped up: "Won't someone offer a seat to this old lady?"[17] Several times, Oma kept Anne and Margot while Edith went to Amsterdam to visit her husband and help select an apartment.

Edith with her daughters Anne (left) and Margot (right) in the center of Frankfurt in 1933. The photo was taken by Otto Frank.

Once Otto had his offices, staff, and supplies in order in December, Edith left Germany forever. The Frank family, German in their speech, customs, and lineage, would have to become Dutch. Rambunctious Anne was left behind with her Oma and her uncles. Edith wisely felt that Margot, sensitive to being uprooted, needed to adjust without her distracting sister. At this time, Edith wrote to their friend Gertrud Naumann: "how well I could use your help with unpacking. . . . Tomorrow both uncles will bring Margot and stay for Christmas. Anne also wants to come. Rosa will have a hard time to keep her there for another couple of weeks."[18] Anne's fond bachelor uncles, Walter and Julius, reportedly enjoyed clowning for their little niece and treated her like royalty.

On her birthday in February 1934, Margot discovered a pretty surprise. All dressed up upon her gift table was her sister Anne. The girls had both become "Amsterdammers."

Germans such as the Franks and the thousands of others who fled Hitler's repression noticed quickly that the Dutch were suspicious of the German government. They frowned on anyone speaking German on the streets. Although Otto and soon the girls developed an ear for the Dutch language, Edith struggled. In the River Quarter where they lived, many other German Jews faced the same problem.

Two German Jewish families, the Goslars and the Ledermanns, became close friends of the Franks. Hanneli "Hanne" Goslar and Suzanne "Sanne" Ledermann became two of Anne's best pals. Barbara Ledermann was Margot's friend. While some immigrant women like Ruth Ledermann had to work, many others were full time mothers who formed coffee circles with Edith Frank. The language barrier between Edith and her husband and children started to grow.

Otto became friends with an immigrant family from Berlin, the Jacobstahls and their daughter Hilde. Hilde stated that her family made a strong effort never to speak German, because the Nazis were so distrusted in the Netherlands.[19] Margot and Anne, bright children playing daily with Dutch companions, soon became fluent Dutch speakers. Only Edith lagged behind, frustrated. After trying private lessons, she gave up and learned what Dutch she could "by osmosis, though so badly that later her children would make fun of her."[20]

The Franks lived in an apartment at 37 Merwedeplein, on a triangular plaza with grass in the center, good for a children's playground.[21] Anne celebrated her fifth birthday in June 1934. At her party was a child several years younger than Anne named Julianne Duke, who lived in an apartment above the Franks. Anne often entertained her younger friend over the next years. When Mrs. Frank invited Julianne and her mother for coffee chats, the child loved "cream cheese sandwiches covered with chocolate sprinkles" and play time with Anne. Julianne said of Anne: "I remember her energy and her laughter . . . she often buttoned my coat, hugged me, pulled me around our horse-shoe shaped street on a small wooden sled. . . ."[22]

In the middle of the Merwedeplein, children from the apartment buildings joined Anne and Margot in games like tag, catch, stick ball, and tumbling, as well as sidewalk activities like hopscotch, jump rope, and roller skating.

Anne continued to thrive in the open atmosphere of the Montessori school program, which let pupils learn in a more self-directed style. Margot, who liked the structure and silence of the regular 1930s classroom, was kept in public school. Anne's early Montessori teacher, Mr. Van Gelder, later recalled speaking with her as they both walked to school each morning:

> . . . she told me stories and poems which she had made up together with her father . . . these were always very jolly stories. She told me a great deal about her father, very little about her sister or her mother . . . in many things she was mature, but in other things she was unusually childish . . . there are many potentialities in such a mixture.[23]

Otto's Office Staff Proves Invaluable

Four employees of the Opetka Amsterdam office turned out to be fine people and invaluable friends. The customer relations assistant was Hermine "Miep" Santrouschitz. In her mid-twenties, Santrouschitz impressed Otto with her energy and intelligence. Santrouschitz was joined by a Dutch secretary named Elizabeth "Bep" Voskuijl. Victor Kugler, an Austrian who like Santrouschitz had emigrated to the Netherlands, had worked for a competing brand of pectin supplies, then became a manager for Opetka. A bookkeeper, Johannes Kleiman, assisted Kugler. This team did everything for the struggling business, such as order the supplies, do the invoices, collect the bills, send out their pectin to the stores that carried it, demonstrate recipes, answer customer questions, and even write the advertising.

Miep Santrouschitz recalled Otto telling her that the pectin "was made from apples—'apple pits,' Mr. Frank joked . . . the housewife combined it with sugar, fresh fruit, and various other ingredients to make her own jam in about ten minutes."[24] Miep, who preferred to be called by her Dutch nickname, practiced every recipe in the office's test kitchen and bragged that her jams turned out perfect.

Soon after Otto and Edith got Anne settled in Amsterdam, Miep enjoyed her first visit with the boss's daughter. Wearing her white furry coat, Anne did not yet speak fluent Dutch. Yet she impressed Miep by understanding all that was going on. Miep showed Anne the office equipment and noticed her curiosity "at things that for us adults were dull and commonplace . . . she looked with fascination at my shiny black typewriter. I held her little fingers to the keys and pressed. Her eyes flashed when the keys jumped and printed black letters."[25] Miep took Anne to the front window, where they might look down on the streetcars, canal boats, bicycles and pedestrians. She recalled how observant the child was, enjoying all the sights below.

A year later, Otto and Edith invited Miep and her boyfriend Jan Gies to dine in their home. Miep told Edith that she sympathized with her, for she too had to struggle to learn the Dutch language as an immigrant girl. Edith must have let down her usual polite reserve with her, for Miep noted: "Mrs. Frank missed Germany a great deal, much more than Mr. Frank . . . she would very often refer with melancholy to their life in Frankfurt."[26] Miep admired the antique furnishings that Edith had brought from Frankfurt, many of which Edith said were part of her wedding dowry.

Anne Does Well at Montessori School

Through her first years in school, Anne continued to grow and thrive mentally. She was an eager student of literature, writing, and drama, but even in her permissive private school, she was considered too much of a chatterbox.

Anne and Margot did household chores for their mother, as they now had no housekeeper. Edith wrote to Gertrud Naumann in June 1935: "the children, whom you taught so well, are helping me."[27] During the warm summer days, the

Frank family took seaside holidays outside Amsterdam with Otto's sister Leni Elias's family from Basel, Switzerland. Anne and Margot loved playing with cousins Stephan and Berndt. Long visits from Oma Hollander also kept the household running smoothly, which Edith, Margot, and Anne greatly appreciated.

In 1935, German Jews had been determined by law to be aliens, unable to vote. A set of edicts called the Nuremberg Laws were passed by the Nazi party and, as historian Michael R. Marrus reports, "Jews were removed from government service, from most professions, and pressured to leave Germany."[28] However, when the summer Olympic Games of 1936 were played in Berlin, Jewish children cheered for German athletes along with everyone else. Being nationalistic had been drummed into the heads and hearts of German Jews for so many centuries it was impossible not to cheer for German Olympians.[29] Adolf Hitler, both chancellor and president, became furious if a "non-Aryan" athlete won a gold medal.

The Nazis Flex Some Military Muscles

Otto Frank may have felt ill at ease about his family's safety in Amsterdam, because during 1937, he took exploratory business trips to Paris and London. No opportunities for resettlement apparently arose. Otto continued to run Opetka in the Netherlands. Just as many Jews feared the Nazis might do, Hitler and the German military forces started expansion plans. Austrian Chancellor Kurt Schuschnigg was forced to give in to the Nazis. Although there had been a large Jewish population in Vienna, "virulent anti-Semitism and economic crisis caused emigration."[30] In March 1938, Nazi troops marched to Vienna, bringing about the Austrian *Anschluss*, or union with

Germany. Confiscation of Jewish property began throughout Austria, just as it had in Germany.

As the Opetka office staff stood by the radio in Amsterdam, the announcer described the masses cheering Hitler's triumphal entry into Vienna, the city where he lived as a young man. Native Austrians Victor Kugler and Miep Santrouschitz were furious to hear that the Austrians put up so little resistance.

News followed of Jewish persecutions in Vienna. Jews were made to scrub the streets and clean public toilets as the Nazis seized their possessions. By September, the Nazi government set its sights on a territory in the present Czechoslovakia. It was called the Sudetenland and bordered Germany. In Munich, prime ministers Neville Chamberlain of Great Britain and Édouard Daladier of France met with Adolf Hitler and his Italian ally, Benito Mussolini. The British and French wanted no part of another world war, so to appease Hitler, they let Germany take over this territory. The Czechs, Slovaks, and Bohemians were quickly subjugated by the Nazis and the ethnic Germans who lived there.[31] Governments in Europe faced the fact that the Nazi forces were gaining strength, and began to make pacts to defend against them.

In the fall of 1938, Anne was nine years old, full of fun, a lover of books, story writing, movie stars, and constant chatting and visiting with girlfriends. The darkening political storm was kept from her and Margot. Former housekeeper Kathi Stilgenbauer wrote Edith Frank that her husband had been imprisoned by the Nazis. Gertrud Naumann let Edith know that her father, a Catholic and liberal democrat, had been fired from his teaching position due to his anti-Nazi politics. Although Edith became increasingly distressed, Otto just worked harder and kept quiet about the Nazi threat.

Miep noted that while Edith was vocal in her bitterness, "Mr. Frank, with his usual nervous quiet manner, kept shaking his head, expressing hope."[32]

Otto took in a business partner, German Jewish refugee Hermann van Pels, an expert on the herbs, spices, and seasonings needed to make sausages. Van Pels, his wife Auguste, and their son Peter lived in the same neighborhood as the Franks and became their friends.

Kristallnacht Unleashes German Pogrom

On November 7, 1938, a Polish Jew shot a German official in Paris over the brutal treatment his parents received from the Nazis. This event was all the Nazis needed to unleash terrorism against German Jews. On November 10, the Franks and their friends the Van Pelses heard radio reports about the previous day's orchestrated attacks. The storm troopers destroyed thousands of Jewish synagogues, businesses, and homes, and killed almost a hundred Jews.[33] Because Jewish businesses and synagogues had their windows shattered before they were ransacked, the attack was called *Kristallnacht*, the Night of Broken Glass. Frankfurt's magnificent synagogue was destroyed, its furniture made into bonfires. The acts of *Kristallnacht* were not a spontaneous popular uprising, as Nazis officials claimed. Historian Michael Marrus stated they were "widely disapproved of [by the German people], mainly because of their hooligan, lawless character, with such wasteful destruction of property."[34]

Otto Frank could not believe that Hitler would extend his conquests into the rest of Europe, or that the German people would support another world war.

A Nazi Invasion

Otto Frank and Hermann van Pels continued to make a living in Amsterdam. Although political turmoil grew throughout Europe and the Soviet Union in 1939, caused by the Nazi party's constant agitation and growing military aggression, the government of the Netherlands remained neutral. Opetka with its pectin business, and Pectacon B.V. with its herbs and spices for sausage making, were holding their own.

In March, Rosa Hollander emigrated from Aachem, Germany, to live with Edith. Anne and Margot adored her. Otto noted: "Oma spoiled the girls, but not unreasonably."[1]

Edith Frank attended religious services at her Reform synagogue and helped with children's festivals. Margot also attended synagogue regularly with her mother and her girlfriends who avidly practiced Judaism.[2] Anne, like Otto, was minimally observant and did not wish to take religious instruction.

Otto made certain both his daughters got his undivided attention and love. Ever since the girls were small, he listened to their schoolwork and problems. Hanneli Goslar recalled Otto even found time to try and teach *her* to ride a bicycle. When Anne at age ten was going through a rebellious stage, Otto told her tales he made up about "Bad Paula" and "Good Paula." Even though Anne was not the embodiment of Bad Paula, Otto wanted her to think about her mistakes and learn to take correction. Knowing that Anne was already interested in writing and loved letters, Otto wrote his thoughts to her during a May 1939 business trip:

> My dear little Anne, things haven't always gone as smoothly for you as they did for your sister, though in general your sense of humor and your amiability allow you to sail through so much so easily. . . . We have agreed on "controls" with each other and you yourself are doing a great deal to swallow the "buts."

Otto said that Anne was a good, decent, loveable girl and was able to laugh soon after the tears and punishments. "May this happy laughter stay with you, the laughter with which you enhance your, our, and other people's lives."[3]

Anne's Summer Fun in 1939

The following summer, Oma Hollander, Anne, and Margot made trips to the seashore, although Oma was unwell and Anne often had colds. A photo shows Anne wrapped tightly in a robe, beside Margot and Oma at the beach. Anne

Anne and Sanne play on Merwedeplein street in 1935. The photo was taken by Otto, whose shadow can be seen in the lower right corner.

captioned it for her diary; "This is June 1939. Margot and I had just got out of the water and I still remember how terribly cold I was. . . . granny sitting there at the back so sweetly and peacefully."[4]

When Anne turned ten on June 12, 1939, her parents threw her a party that included picnicking in a nearby park. Her Jewish friends Hannelies "Hanne" Goslar and Suzanne "Sanne" Ledermann, along with some non-Jewish school friends, were invited.[5] These girlfriends were allowed to attend each other's parties, ride bikes, play games together, and meet at their favorite shops. Still small, Anne was discovering the fascinating subjects of boys and social life.

Although the Franks' family funds were barely ample, the family seemed secure. The girls did a lot of the housework, and the upstairs room was rented out for extra cash. That summer, Edith wrote to Gertrud Naumann, "my husband is in desperate need of a few day's rest. The business is a constant struggle but otherwise things are going smoothly for us."[6]

The Third Reich Threatens Europe

While Anne and Margot concentrated on poetry, math, friendships, movie stars, the royal family, and hairdos, their parents tried to look ahead. As Anne and Margot went to class that September 1939, the armies of the Third Reich under Adolf Hitler attacked Poland. The British and the French had pacts to defend Poland's freedom. "German victory over Poland, aided by the Soviet invasion, was achieved in only five weeks."[7] When Hitler ignored these western nations, Great Britain and France were forced to declare war. As Hitler's armed forces secured Poland, all its over 2 million Jews fell under his control. The former nation was carved into German and Soviet territories. Although Otto Frank could foresee

Jewish repression now following in Poland, he believed that the Netherlands was neutral and would be safe.

The Jews Struggle in the Netherlands

By 1939, scholars estimate that in Germany, Austria, and Czechoslovakia, "an estimated 975,000 members of the Jewish religious community had . . . come under Nazi control."[8] Many Jews had already emigrated to France, Great Britain, the Netherlands, Palestine, and the United States. Estimates of refugees into the Netherlands vary, between 17,000 to 25,000, with 20 percent unemployed. They relied on relief organizations like the *Comite Voor Joodsche Vluchtelingen*, or CJV, which got its money from "major international Jewish charities and collections made within the Netherlands."[9] From March 1933 to March 1940, the CJV raised all the money needed to help refugees with relocation needs.

That spring, all immigrants had to register with the Dutch Office for Resident Foreigners. Otto registered his family, as did Hermann van Pels. Otto decided their business was growing and needed a larger office and warehouse facility. They moved down to 263 Prinsengracht, an industrial area of old brick buildings. Miep Santrouschitz described the place as facing a canal with three front doors on street level: the first door led up to storage rooms ". . . that we didn't have any need to explore or to use right away;" the next door to a landing which led to all the offices and workrooms, and the third door "led to the street-level work area."[10]

Anne's Growth Spurt and Recovered Health

Miep noted how Anne's arms and legs were stretching out that spring, and how she developed a skill of mimicry and clowning. As a fifth-year student in 1940 at Montessori

School, Anne was taught by Miss Gadron, and in her sixth year in 1941 by the head of school, Mrs. Kuperus. Mrs. Kuperus later recalled how Anne "had been ill for a while, but recovered nicely . . . ," and participated in drama, reading, and had lots of friends. "She had a great team spirit and really enjoyed working in groups."[11] Family friend Isa Baschwitz later stated: "I used to go around mainly with Margot, who was three years younger than I. Anne was a very vivacious girl who, because she had a heart condition, was rather pampered and spoiled . . ."[12]

Anne and Margot became pen pals with two American sisters, Juanita and Betty Ann Wagner from Danville, Iowa. The teacher of the Wagner girls, Miss Birdie Mathews, traveled to Europe in 1939 and met Montessori teachers who agreed to a pen pal project. Although the letters from the Wagners have not survived, Anne and Margot's letters from April 1940 are preserved. "It is believed that Anne's first draft was in Dutch, and then her father . . . translated the words and had her redo the letter in English." Anne also enclosed a letter from Margot, addressed to Juanita's sister, Betty; photographs of themselves; and a picture postcard.[13] It appears that Juanita wrote to Anne about the American school system and her mother, who was a teacher, for Anne replied in her letter: "We have no hour-classes we may do what we prefer, of course we must get to a certain goal. Your mother will certainly know this system, it is called Montessori. We have little work at home."[14]

Anne said she had located the town of Burlington, Iowa (near Danville) on the map. Regarding the postcard of Amsterdam that she included, she told Juanita that she had a collection of about 800 cards and would continue collecting. Anne asked Juanita and Betty to send photos, as she was curious to see how they looked. She also asked for their birth dates and said she'd include the address of another girlfriend (Suzanne Ledermann) who wanted a pen pal: "Hoping to hear from you I remain your Dutch friend Annelies Marie Frank."

Margot wrote to Betty Ann, explaining that, "during the week I am very busy as I have to work for school at home every day."[15] Since Margot was in a traditional school, she had more home assignments. "Wednesday and Saturday afternoon we are free and use our time to play tennis and to row. In the winter we play hockey or go skating . . ." Margot must have been asked about the political situation, because she replied that "having a frontier with Germany and being a small country we never feel safe." Margot explained that their only cousins were in Basel, Switzerland, which was a difficult trip for them, due to strict travel restrictions: "It is war and no visas are given."[16] She described their five-room apartment and the flat low land surrounding Amsterdam.

Juanita and Betty Ann Wagner sent letters and photos back to the Franks. Along with their teacher, they waited for responses. The Wagners did not know that the Franks were Jewish, nor did they realize the difference that was soon to make in their lives. In their isolated Iowa farmhouse, which had neither a television or radio in 1940, the Wagners did not understand the onslaught of Naziism in Europe.

Erich and Elfriede Geiringer, also Jewish immigrants, moved into Merwedeplein at the beginning of 1940. Their daughter Eva was Anne's age, and their son Heinz was put in class with Margot. Eva was instantly attracted to Suzanne Ledermann, her neighbor, and wanted to be part of the trio of Sanne, Hanne, and Anne. She noted that each of the trio were "a little more sophisticated than the rest of us—more like teenagers."[17] Sanne Ledermann did befriend Eva, and told her "how much she admired her friend Anne Frank because she was so stylish."[18]

Once when Eva's mother took her to the dressmaker, she heard a young client instructing the lady to make larger shoulder pads, and the hemline should be just a little higher, don't you think? The curtains opened, and there stood Anne, alone, making her fashion decisions. Eva was breathless with envy as Anne twirled and showed off her new peach-colored frock, or dress.[19]

When Eva was invited to get-togethers in the Frank apartment, her favorite activity was to pet Anne's large cat and drink Edith's lemonade while admiring Sanne and Anne. Heinz Geiringer and Margot became good friends and did homework together.

Otto Fears Nazi Invasion

Otto continued to correspond by mail with relatives in Germany and with cousins in London. Cousin Milly said that Otto became their go-between for information. When he wrote of his fears of a Nazi attack on the Netherlands, Milly and her mother immediately made him an offer. They would take Anne and Margot into their home in Great Britain for as long as the war lasted. Otto wrote back: "Edith and I discussed your letter. We both feel we simply can't do it. We couldn't bear to part with the girls. They mean too much to us."[20]

As it turned out, the Franks might not have had time to get their daughters safely transported to Britain. On April 9, 1940, two German divisions moved into Denmark, taking Copenhagen in only 12 hours of battle. The German forces also landed in Norway, where the British sent troops to support the local army. Due to German air superiority and battleship plans of attack, they succeeded in defeating the British troops. By the end of April, Germany drove the British from Norway. German forces bombed Belgium in May, and sent in land divisions. World War II scholar Donald Sommerville stated that "neither the Belgians or the Dutch [have given] the Allies any real cooperation in planning a joint defense" because they wanted to remain neutral in hopes of avoiding German attack.[21] The plan failed totally. Within hours, German forces also invaded the Netherlands.

Miep stood with Otto Frank and the staff by the radio throughout May 10, 1940. She noted: "Mr. Frank's face was white. . . . It seemed that our brave Dutch Army was fighting on . . . and that we were making a stand."[22] Confusion and unfounded reports flew for days. Then came the news: members of the Dutch royal family had escaped by ship to England, taking all the gold from the treasury. By May 14, the Dutch general announced "the Germans had obliterated Rotterdam with bombs dropped from the air; . . . the Germans had threatened to bomb Utrecht and Amsterdam if we continued to resist."[23] Surrender was the only option.

Suddenly the Netherlands was divided into two camps: Nazi sympathizers and cooperators on one side, and loyal Dutch who opposed occupation until death. Miep and her fiancé Jan Gies would side against the Nazis and fight in their own way for freedom.

Frank and Van Pels Become Silent Partners

Of the approximately one hundred-forty thousand Jews living in the Netherlands in 1940, 60 percent lived in Amsterdam. Reich Commissioner Arthur Seyss-Inquart, with his SS police force ruled the Netherlands. Knowing that the Jewish persecution going on in Germany, Austria, Poland, and other places would soon come to the Netherlands, Otto Frank put his business into the names of several trusted Dutch Christians. He created a cover company, and made Jan Gies

The Dutch Royal Family

Dutch royalty, known as the House of Orange, was an ancient and respected monarchy. Both males and females were equally in line for the throne. Wilhelmina had been Queen since 1890 when she reached the throne as a ten-year-old child. She reigned with her husband, Prince Hendrik. Her only daughter Princess Juliana married Prince Bernhard in 1937, and gave birth to Princess Beatrix in 1938 and Princess Irene in 1939.[24]

By taking the gold from the treasury to England in May 1940, Queen Wilhelmina and her family could keep ruling the country from abroad. While in exile in 1943, Princess Margriet was born.

The British government enabled the Dutch royal family to broadcast to their subjects in the Netherlands, keeping them updated and determined. Anne, who had admired and adored the royals, pasted her photos of them on her wall. She listened avidly when the Queen's voice was heard, for she missed them in their absence. After occupation ended, the Dutch royal family returned to their quarters in The Hague, the seat of the royal court, to help their nation recover. Queen Beatrix's eldest child Crown Prince Willem-Alexander is heir to the Dutch throne.

the supervisory director, and Victor Kugler the managing director. Although he was the actual owner, the business now looked non-Jewish.[25] Otto faced the fact that getting himself, Edith, Oma Hollander, and the two girls all visas to emigrate to America, England, or Switzerland was now impossible. He would have to stay among the Dutch, keep smiling, and be very careful.

Sanne and Barbara Ledermann's father Franz did not wait for his apartment to be searched for literature by banned authors. He took the books he had brought from Germany and held his own private bonfire.[26]

Anne and Hanne still had girlish fun. Their favorite weekend activity was to go to Otto's offices and play office worker. They would phone each other on the intercoms, type letters, use stamps, and even mischievously pour water on passerbys from the second floor windows! Miep and Bep loved hearing the girls giggle at their pranks, for there was so little to laugh about during Nazi occupation. In October 1940, Margot and Anne went often to Hanne's to play with the new baby Rachel Gabriele. Margot wrote to her Grandmother Frank in Basel: "Anne and I love to go visit the Goslars' baby . . . she laughs now and grows cuter by the day." Anne, now eleven, also wrote to Oma Hollander about her school life, and confessed that during her dictation class she "made no less than 27 mistakes."[27]

Anne's teacher Mrs. Kuperus had the sixth graders do original theatricals. The head script person and lead player was usually Anne. She said: "Anne was in her element . . . the big parts fell to her." Although Anne was still petite, when she played the queen, "she suddenly seemed a good bit taller than the others."[28]

Nazis Begin Jewish Repression in the Netherlands

By February 1941, anti-Jewish legislation moved into the Netherlands. As Margot passed her fifteenth birthday, and Anne posed for photos with friends Hermann and Herbert Wilp, their social lives suddenly changed. Jews were not permitted in movie theaters, which was a blow to Anne. That spring, they were forbidden from enjoying public beaches and pools, parks, spas, and sporting arenas.

The Nazi war machine moved on, with Germany taking control of Yugoslavia. Italy, Hitler's ally, conquered Greece. Jews could only work in Jewish companies of which there were a dwindling few. That spring, thirty thousand Dutch men volunteered to join the German Waffen SS, intending to fight communism in Eastern Europe. Still, Anne and her friends tried to live an almost normal life. They skated in outdoor rinks, played games, and passed around photo and poem albums. Hanne recalled that Anne had more boys' signatures in her books than girls, and was an avid writer in diaries.

Jews were soon forbidden to go to school with non-Jewish children. Mrs. Kuperus recalled sadly how they had to let eighty-seven pupils go from the Montessori School. "It was not until this happened that we realized how many Jewish children we had had. . . . In Anne's class alone there were twenty."[29] No difference had ever been made in treatment of the pupils. Starting in September, Anne and Margot would be sent to a school called the Jewish Lyceum. "Lyceum" means academy. Mrs. Kuperus said Anne wept when she had to say goodbye to her teacher.

The summer of 1941 was made bearable for Anne by a holiday with Sanne and the Ledermanns in their relatives' country house. "We sleep a lot better at night here than in Amsterdam," Anne wrote to Grandmother Frank. Air raid sirens roused Anne almost nightly in Amsterdam, for the British Royal Air Force bombers roared overhead towards military targets. "I'm reading a lot," Anne wrote to Otto, "and have read all my books and Sanne's books. . ."[30]

Later in the holiday with Sanne, Anne must have gotten a care package, for she wrote her parents: "Many thanks for the two film-star cards," and a treat of sugar, jam and rice, which she ate a great deal of to settle her upset stomach and headache.[31] Anne and Margot were facing a strange new school, a repressive, anti-Semitic life in their city, and an uncertain, wartorn world. They were no longer able to write freely to the Wagner sisters in Danville, Iowa, who waited in confusion. It is no wonder Anne's stomach was upset.

Romance Triumphs

One beautiful thing happened in Anne's troubled world: Miep and Jan Gies had their wedding in July. Earlier, when Miep and Jan were entertained at the Frank's home, Miep noticed Anne's usual conversations about her anger at the anti-Jewish laws, her favorite film stars, and her best girlfriends, now contained "chatter about particular young people of the opposite sex."[32] Miep's wedding was a simple ceremony at City Hall on July 16. They were joined by such friends as Bep Voskuijl, Mr. and Mrs. Van Pels, and Anne and Otto Frank. "Anne looked very grown-up indeed in her princess-style coat and matching hat with a ribbon around the brim. Anne's hair had grown longer," Miep noted, and shown thick and shiny from her constant brushing.[33] Later, Otto and Hermann threw a reception for Miep and Jan at their offices, where they were presented with lovely gifts. Anne performed the role of delighted hostess. For that moment, romantic dreams of love and marriage were what filled her young heart.

45

4

Amsterdam in the Nazis' Grasp

Pressure was put on Otto Frank and Hermann van Pels in 1941 to trade with the *Wehrmacht*, the name the Nazis gave to their army. Those who refused would get shut down. Since the Nazis occupying the Netherlands assumed that Opetka was a non-Jewish company, they also expected that the company would trade with them and get their supplies through government-approved channels. Almost 80 percent of Dutch businesses depended on German officials and their brokers for their supplies and traded with the Wehrmacht.[1] Miep said that Otto would call himself adviser but continued to run the business. "He . . . made all the decisions and gave all the orders . . ." said Miep, and when time came to sign an order or a check, Kugler or Kleiman . . . gave their "totally Christian signature."[2]

Miep later stated that during 1941–1942 "there were deliveries. The agreements were made by Kleiman. There was no choice—no delivery could mean the closing down of the company."[3] As to why the German government wanted pectin, no one can be sure. Besides preserving jams and food products, pectin was a thickener. Certain kinds were used for "raising blood volume in blood transfusions."[4] Otto and Hermann would have no way of knowing if they were serving the German armed forces. Even to speak badly of any Nazi could result in a Dutch person's arrest. Otto cooperated with the Wehrmacht to protect his business. He believed this was the only way to feed his family.

The Nazi regime, under the direction of the *Führer*, meaning leader, Adolf Hitler, kept its same goals and leaders since it took over in 1934. Heinrich Himmler was head of the SS, and the secret state police, also called the Gestapo. Hermann Göring was the prime minister; and Joseph Goebbels was the propaganda minister.[5] The Nazis put in place a state intelligence service to find any political opponents, and within one year, over twenty-five thousand political prisoners were sent to prison camps such as the one at Dachau, along with actual criminals.[6] The concentration camp system grew throughout the 1930s, suppressing serious opposition to the Nazi regime.

New Jewish School, New Friends

In the fall of 1941, Anne Frank underwent a traumatic transition in her life by transferring with Margot to the Jewish Lyceum. Eva Geiringer said her parents decided to send her brother Heinz to the Lyceum with Margot, but preferred hiring a tutor to teach Eva in the home. The Geiringers asked Otto and Edith to let Anne join the home schooling class, but they declined.[7] Anne made the best of her new school. A classmate Laureen Klein stated that she rode the same streetcar to school as Anne did: "Anne and her entourage would get on the street

car and I would think, 'Isn't she lively?' She definitely was the center of the circle. Talk, talk!"[8]

Many Jewish students felt embarrassed to be forced from their old schools into the Lyceum. One of them was Salvador Bloemgarten, age sixteen, who went to class with Margot. Soon, he realized their education was excellent, and he was having "a wonderful year . . . All the assimilated Jews felt very comfortable with each other, there was a good atmosphere, and we had good teachers."[9]

Anne had been lonely in her new class, knowing no one and being separated from Hanne. She did what Anne did best: chattered so much that the teacher relented and sent her to join Hanne's class. The Lyceum was far more strict and structured than the Montessori system, but Anne would later admit "I was reconciled to the school, . . . where I was to have so much fun and learn such a lot."[10]

Anne as Babysitter

The Kohnstam family lived on the first floor of the Frank's apartment building. Also German Jewish refugees, Mr. and Mrs. Kohnstam had one son, Pieter, seven years younger than Anne. During after school hours, or when the Kohnstams and the Franks played bridge in the evening, Anne would look after little Pieter. "I was five years old in 1941," Pieter Kohnstam recalled, "and Anne would come to our apartment frequently.

Anne stands second from left with the dark print dress. Sanne and Hanne are to the right of Anne, respectively. The photo was taken by Otto Frank on Anne's 10th birthday—June 12, 1939.

She was an outgoing, bubbly girl. . . Anne liked to get out of the house." Pieter enjoyed playing games on the sidewalk and sandy playground with Anne and her friends. By 1942, when Pieter was six, he recalled that he and Anne realized that the Nazi police were coming into their neighborhood. "We saw people being taken away, Anne and I," Pieter stated.[11]

Bicycling around the city was popular with the Dutch of all ages. Riding home from school one day, Anne pedaled after a girl she had noticed in class: Jacqueline van Maarsen. Jacqueline was supposed to have gone to Girls High, but being half Jewish, she was forced to transfer to the Lyceum, where she had few friends. Anne befriended her, nicknaming her Jacque, or Jopie, a popular Dutch name.

Jacque recalled that along with Sanne and Hanne, Anne created a circle of friends for doing homework and playing games. "Anne and I shared the same interests," Jacque said. "We did our homework together, which really amounted to my helping her with math . . . I thought it was nonsense to study geography and history when you could look up everything anyway. As a result I received some 'unsatisfactories' while the diligent Anne excelled."[12] Recreation centered around home activities, since Jews were forbidden to go almost every place and curfew for them was 8 P.M. Jacque recalled that Monopoly games were the girls' favorite, where she and Anne and Sanne and Hanne would be joined by Margot and Jacque's older sister Christiane.

Movie Fun at the Franks

Collections of film star photos were a passion for both Anne, and Jacque, who said: "My movie star collection was much smaller than Anne's—my only idols were Deanne (sic) Durbin and Shirley Temple, while Anne also had many UFA [a German film company] stars."[13] Germans in the 1930s enjoyed both films made in their own studios and ones from Hollywood, with German translations. Occasionally Otto managed to rent films for private home parties for Anne and Margot's friends. Jacque and Anne soon got into the spirit of the cinema, and made invitations that were make-believe tickets, which stated "Without this card, no entrance. Please inform in time. Row __, Seat ___."[14] Jacque and Anne would let any of their friends come, but the tickets made the dream of going to the movies seem to be really happening.

Although Otto and Edith kept their home open to their daughters' friends of all religions, Anne found it harder to see her Christian friends. She'd been pals with Lucia van Dijk and Ietje Swillens. Now Lucia's parents had joined the Dutch National Socialist Movement (NSB). They insisted Lucia belong to the *Jeugdstorm* (Youth Storm), the Dutch version of the Association (League) of German Girls. The Nazis made attendance for children of party members mandatory.[15] Lucia's father was unemployed and the family clung to the hope that the National Socialists would create jobs.[16] Therefore Lucia and Anne became isolated from each other.

Work Begins on the Final Solution

While the Frank sisters had good schooling, with a restricted social and cultural life, their parents hid their fears about what the occupational government was planning for Jews. The term Final Solution (*Endlosung* in German) was one used by Nazi authorities to refer to "massive forced emigration of Jews" to foreign countries such as Madagascar.[17] By the first half of 1941, the Nazis were changing the meaning of the term Final Solution. During July 1941, Prime Minister Hermann Göring wrote to Reinhard Heydrich, head of a branch of the SS, to begin preparations for a "total solution of the Jewish question." On August 28, Adolf Eichmann, an SS official, wrote about an imminent final solution as "now in preparation."[18] Historians have no written record of what Adolf Hitler meant by the Final Solution, yet his officers must have had instructions from him to continue pursuing this policy. Jews had been transported to camps, mostly in Poland since its occupation by the Nazis. It is probable that Hitler's decision to try to exterminate Europe's Jews came between September and November 1941.[19]

All non-Dutch Jews living in the Netherlands were forced to register in December 1941 at an agency called the *Zentralstelle fur Judische Auswanderung* (Central Agency for Jewish Emigration). It seemed wise to quietly comply. Otto went alone, keeping this registration for voluntary emigration to himself.[20]

United States Enters the War

On December 7, an unexpected event happened. Japan attacked the United States military bases at Pearl Harbor, Hawaii. The United States declared war. Since Germany and Japan were allied, Germany had to declare war on the United States. The Franks and their friends drank in this exciting news. Miep Gies said: "our spirits rose . . . it was almost unbelievable: America, with all its manpower and airplane factories, was now allied with England against our oppressors . . . with us in this fight against Hitler."[21]

Chanukah Theatrical Stars Anne Frank

The Franks and other Jewish families got together, hired a director, and let their children put on a play for Chanukah. This annual eight-day festival celebrates the victory of the Jewish Maccabees over the Syrians and the rededication of the temple in Jerusalem in 165 B.C. Along with gift giving, prayers, and the lighting of the festival prayer candles each evening, songs and dramas are often performed. Anne was thrilled to win the title role of *The Princess with the Long Nose!* The show was put on in the apartment of her friend Hannelore Klein, using the dining room as the stage area, and the living room packed with an audience of family and friends.[22] Anne's role was that of a beautiful but arrogant princess who snacked on a forbidden magic cake, only to sprout an ugly nose. After humbling herself and asking forgiveness, her beauty was restored.

While the Franks were celebrating their religious festival at the end of 1941, a secret balance sheet was being prepared by the chief of the SS in the Netherlands, regarding the nation's Jewish situation:

"Hostages currently on hand: 238. Arrestees awaiting criminal trial: 1433. Jews delivered to reception camp: 1354. Survivors of 900 Jews deported to Mauthausen in the course of the year: 8. Total (in captivity): 3033."[23] The list was a predictor of the terrible future awaiting the Jewish population of the Netherlands.

To organize their plans for murder, the Nazis held a critical meeting on January 20, 1942, at Wannsee, a villa in Berlin. Fifteen officials represented the German state ministries. Wilhelm Stuckart had drafted the 1935 Nuremberg Laws, which removed all freedoms of citizenship from Jews. Freidrich Kritzinger represented Hitler's own office called the Reich Chancellery. Gestapo chief Heinrich Muller, and SD leader Reinhard Heydrich, along with second in command Adolf Eichmann, represented the intelligence branch responsible for arresting Jews and putting them in camps. Erich Neuman, heading the office of labor supply and war production, "pointed out the serious economic consequences of eliminating a labor force now that the war had taken a turn

Adolf Eichmann

Born in 1906 in Solingen, Germany, Adolf Eichmann failed both regular high school and vocational school for engineering after his family moved to Austria. "The profession that appears on his official documents: construction engineer, had as much connection with reality as the statement that his birthplace was Palestine and that he was fluent in Hebrew and Yiddish," said historian Hannah Erendt.[24]

After working as a salesman, in 1933 Eichmann was hired by the SD, or Office for Reich Security, as an internal spy for the Nazis. By 1937, he was considered an expert on "the organizational methods and ideology of Jewry, the enemy," by his bosses.[25] After Germany annexed Austria in March 1938, Eichmann's job was to oversee the expulsion of all Austrian Jews. He rose in the Nazi ranks, directly under Reinhard Heydrich, head of the SD.

Hitler's policy changed from expulsion of Jews to extermination. Then, stated historian Peter Z. Malkin, "Eichmann saw his mission, the elimination of Jews from the face of the earth, as a priority at least equal to that of winning the war."[26] Coordinating the efforts of the SS and local police in all occupied states, Eichmann tried to ensure that every Jew was identified and imprisoned in a camp. He referred to his policies as "dejudaization measures."[27]

for the worse."[28] No one accepted Neuman's concept of saving the Jews to use as essential, enslaved workers. The peculiar reasoning of Josef Buhler, who argued for removal because "the Jew constitutes a substantial danger as carrier of epidemics," won over at Wannsee.[29]

Reinhard Heydrich, who worked directly with Heinrich Himmler, achieved his objectives at the Wannsee Conference: killing Jews was the accepted policy of the German state, and death by gassing became the preferred method at the six death camps in German-occupied Poland.[30] Already in Poland, captives labored in six thousand camps; in Germany even more were in operation.[31] Because most means of communication were controlled by the Nazis, the Jews in the Netherlands had no clear idea about these facts.

Anne Grows into Adolescence

Anne had her first experience with death that January, when her beloved Oma Hollander died of cancer. Anne and the entire Frank family grieved for her.

Anne, however, was irrepressible at age twelve, and kept her school and social life in high gear. When her girlfriend Ilse Wagner got a table-tennis table, a girl's club was formed: Sanne as president, Jacque as secretary, and Hanne, Ilse, and Anne as the members. As Jacque noted, the club was fun because "there was so little we were allowed to do."[32] Table-tennis tournaments filled the girls' need for recreation and gossiping about boys and the other people that they knew.

Sexual awakening and the facts of reproduction became of utmost interest to Anne as she approached her thirteenth birthday. Jacque was amused that Anne had come up with lots of misinformation about sex, for Edith and Margot would not go into detail. Jacque's mother, a French high-fashion seamstress, and her older sister, were more open about the facts of life. Jacque and Anne enjoyed frequent sleepovers during the winter term of 1942, to which Anne always brought a little overnight case with her curlers, hairbrush, and combing cape which caught any loose hairs. She had taken to wearing one of Margot's bras stuffed with cotton. During sleepovers, Anne got Jacque to reveal all she knew about relations between men and women. Jacque recalled that Anne: ". . . made everything fun. I have never met anyone else since then who enjoyed life as completely as my friend Anne did."[33]

Amsterdam Becomes a War Zone

Life in 1942 grew harder in the Netherlands. Air raids, food shortages, supplies being drained from the Netherlands to Germany, all took their toll on the Dutch. Blackout screens for the windows went up each evening. Ration books had been issued for all necessities. In 1941, all Dutch citizens were required to carry an identification card; however, the Jewish citizens had a huge "J" stamped in the center of theirs.[34]

In April 1942, a mandate came from the Dutch Nazi government that had already been in operation for a year in Germany: all Jews over the age of six had to wear a yellow Star of David sewn on every item of clothing. Each star bore the word Jood, which meant "Jew." Peter Levi, then a young boy, recalled: "You could buy them in the shop professionally made, but [Mother] found some yellow fabric and vaguely made one herself. My friends . . . sported nice, shiny shop-bought yellow stars which I thought were far more interesting."[35] To Bertje Block-van Rhijn, the star as a branding device became apparent: "I didn't realize at first what it was, but I began to detest it gradually. All those NSB [Dutch Nazi Party] people! . . . I started to think about it. That a lot of people would be very nice and that the NSB would yell after me, Yid, dirty Yid!"[36] "Yid" was an offensive term that referred to a Jewish-spoken language called Yiddish.

Irene Butter-Hasenberg, age eleven, noticed that "the way the Dutch people responded to this edict that all the Jews had to wear stars was that large numbers of gentile people wore the star in the beginning. They felt that if everybody wore the star, it would defeat the purpose. Then . . . measures were taken against that."[37] Jacque van Maarsen said: "We became instantly recognizable. . . . By accident I sat on a bench in the square, after that was no longer allowed, and almost walked into a store no longer open to Jews. One could be picked up for such offenses."[38]

Miep Gies, along with all righteous liberal Dutch, was furious on behalf of her friends. She noted that many Christians also sewed yellow stars to their coats, or wore yellow flowers in lapels, to show their support. Gies said that when Otto came to the office with "the yellow star affixed by neat stitches to his coat. No attention was paid. We looked through it as though it were not there. To me, it was not."[39] Mandatory prison sentences for any non-Jew wearing a star put a stop to shows of solidarity.

5

The Franks Go Into Hiding

In 1942, young Jews in the Netherlands were being called up to work in German labor camps. Otto and Edith kept silent about it, wanting their daughters to stay carefree as long as possible. Anne did not seem to worry about things disappearing from the family's apartment. However, observant Jacque van Maarsen did. "It struck me one day that all of the chairs had disappeared from the living room and there were different chairs about the table . . . the reply was, 'They've been sent away to be reupholstered.' . . . I had always thought the chairs looked nice, but I kept my mouth shut."[1] Otto and Edith were storing things gradually with the Kleimans and others, apparently making plans to vanish in the near future.

That spring Anne wrote to her Grandmother Frank in Basel, "I'm still enjoying the lyceum. There are 12 girls and 18 boys in our class. At first we ran around with the boys a lot, but now we're not and it's a good thing, because they're getting too fresh."[2] Hanneli and Jacque noticed Anne writing a lot in a journal but shielding them from seeing her entries.

Clinging to Normalcy

British bombers regularly flew the night skies over the Netherlands in 1942. They targeted German occupation installations in the Netherlands, or continued over land to targets in Germany. Amsterdam was put on alert by air raid sirens or alarms. The Franks took shelter in areas like stone archways or cellars; their house darkened with blackout screens on the windows. Toosje, a girlfriend of Anne's, said that the "searchlights were passing across the sky, and the anti-aircrafts boomed and flashed, and Anne was standing beside me, the star on her breast, and we were all . . . terribly frightened . . ." Their neighbor Dr. Beffie stood beside them, slowly chewing a piece of bread. "Anne could not help staring at him, no matter how frightened she was. And once, just as the all clear came, Anne said to me: 'Dear God, if I chewed so slowly I think I'd be hungry all my life.'"[3]

War Rumors

Hanne Goslar reported that her father Hans disagreed with Otto about where the war was heading. Hans was "convinced the Germans would win the war and kill all the Jews." Otto believed that with the efforts of the British and the Americans, the madness would be ended before it was too late.[4]

When the Nazis sent another round of call-up notices, dark stories spread about these labor camps. Were they merely factories? "To maintain this charade, the Germans allowed Dutch Jews to send mail and packages to those in the camps . . . most people could not imagine that their family members . . . were being annihilated simply because they were Jews."[5] According to historian Hedda Rosner Kopf, the camps began as pools of forced labor. Kopf goes on to say:

> . . . killing became a distinct function of the system. . . .
> In the autumn of 1941, the first experiments with the
> deadly Zyklon B gas were undertaken at Auschwitz, . . .
> Shortly after, gassings occurred at Chelmno . . . in
> western Poland. Systematic killings on a similar model
> followed at Belzec, Sobibor, and Treblinka in 1942.[6]

However, most Dutch Jews did not believe these rumors of mass executions.

Anne was able to briefly forget the war on June 12, her birthday, when she received many gifts. Her favorite was one she had requested: a red checkered diary. Her party that Sunday, June 14, was well attended by her best friends, including Hanne and Jacque, as well as Margot and her friend Jetteke. The girls recalled Anne's eyes sparkling with delight over her presents. Edith and Otto served strawberry tart and milk to all.[7] The grand entertainment was a showing of the film *Rin-Tin-Tin and the Lighthouse Keeper*. Anne, who loved animals, was a fan of Rin-Tin-Tin, the famed German Shepherd star of Hollywood.

Otto Confesses His Secret Plan

In June 1942, Anne complained to her journal: "We are all positively melting, and in this heat I have to go on foot everywhere. Now I can fully appreciate how nice a tram is, but that is a forbidden luxury for Jews."[8] Miep Gies noted:

> Although Mr. Frank gave the impression of everything's
> being normal, I could see he was worn out . . . he had to
> walk many miles to the office each day, and then return
> home on foot at night. It was impossible for me to
> imagine the strain that he, Mrs. Frank, Margot, and
> Anne were under.[9]

Otto and Edith had been quietly transporting items into a chosen hiding space. Miep stated that when Otto asked her to help, she never backed away. The Franks and the Van Pels would go into hiding in second and third floor empty rooms that were sealed off at the rear of their office building. The office would go on working below them. The staff would have to be fearless in case Nazi officers came to question them.

Miep said that Otto then asked her:

> "Miep, are you willing to take on the responsibility of taking care of us while we are in hiding?"
>
> "Of course," I answered.
>
> "Miep, for those who help Jews, the punishment is harsh."
>
> I said, "Of course." I meant it.[10]

During June 1942, Anne and Margot completed their term in school and looked forward to relaxing. As Anne and her classmates wrote in their yearbooks, wishing each other happy lives and wonderful summers, they assumed they would be together when the Lyceum resumed in the fall. Anne invited her friend Helmuth "Hello" Silberberg to have dessert with her family. Although three years older than Anne, Hello had a crush on her. He reflected: "She was fascinating. Articulate. I wasn't used to that intellect in one so young."[11] She wrote to Kitty, her nickname for her diary, "I had bought a cream cake, sweets, and tea and fancy biscuits. . . . Neither Hello nor I felt like sitting stiffly side by side indefinitely, so we went for a walk and it was already ten past eight when he brought me home. Daddy was very cross."[12]

Otto had good reason to be furious, for Jewish teenagers caught out after the 8:00 P.M. curfew might be rounded up and sent to Westerbork, the Dutch holding camp. Otto made Anne swear to be more careful.

Hermine 'Miep' Santrouschitz Gies

Although her Austrian name was Hermine, her Dutch foster parents called her Miep. As an Austrian child, Miep became so ill from malnutrition during World War I that when the war ended, her country sent her and others to the Netherlands to recuperate. Miep grew to be robust, a good student, and identified with the values of the Dutch. She and her foster family lived in the River Quarter of Amsterdam, near the Franks' home. Otto Frank hired Miep as his assistant, partly because she could speak both German and Dutch. Miep stated her political view: "I disapproved of the fanatic Adolf Hitler, who had recently seized power in Germany."[13] Miep became an indispensable worker and, along with her fiancé Jan Gies, part of the Frank family's social circle.

When the time came, Miep and Jan Gies risked their lives to support their friends who went in hiding. Later Miep said of herself: "I am not a hero. I stand at the end of the long, long line of good Dutch people who did what I did or more— much more—during those dark and terrible times."[14] Miep was appointed a Knight of the Order of Oranje-Nassau by the Queen for her courage. She also received the Order of Merit of the Federal Republic of Germany in 1994, and the Righteous Among the Nations award by Yad Vashem.[15]

On July 1, Anne sat home, bored and waiting for Hello to call. At six, she answered the phone and heard: "This is Helmuth Silberberg. May I please speak to Anne?" Politely he said he could not spend the evening with her, but wanted to come by for a quick visit. As the couple strolled together, Hello announced that his grandparents insisted Anne was too young to be a girlfriend. However, he had a plan: instead of going to his Zionist Club meetings during Wednesday, Saturday, and Sunday afternoons, he could come around and be with her. Anne protested he should not go behind his grandparents' backs, to which Hello replied: "Love finds a way."[16] Regarding the teasing her friend Jacque gave her about Hello, Anne said: "I'm honestly not in love, oh, no, I can surely have boy friends."[17]

The Dreaded Call-up Comes

Anne's carefree days came to an end on the morning of July 5. Otto told her the family had been secretly hiding food, clothes, and furniture for more than a year. Soon their family must go into hiding. That day, as Anne was sunbathing on their roof, Margot ran up: "'The S.S. have sent a call-up notice for Daddy . . . Of course he won't go,' declared Margot while we waited together. 'Mummy has gone to the v.P.s [Van Pelses] to ask whether we should move into our hiding place tomorrow. The v.P.s are going with us, there will be 7 of us in all."[18] Soon Margot confessed the truth: The SS call-up notice was for herself. Terrified, Anne burst into tears. If they did not go into hiding immediately, Margot would be taken away.

Heinz Geiringer received a call-up notice at the same time. His sister Eva said: "it gave instructions for him to report with a rucksack in three days' time to the old theatre nearby." Heinz offered to go, saying his friends Henk, Marcel, and Margot had their cards too, "so we will all be together."[19]

Erich Geiringer, not so naïve, announced that the family would disappear within 24 hours. Heinz and Margot never saw each other to say goodbye.

Edith alerted the Van Pelses; Otto called Johannes Kleiman. Hermann van Pels, included in the plan, told Miep: "they're in a state of great confusion. There's so much to do and so little time, and their damned lodger seems to be hanging about, making it all quite difficult."[20] Mr. Goldschmidt, the single gentleman who rented the third floor room over the Franks', picked that evening to arrive for a chat. Kleiman, Miep, and Jan went to the Franks', where Miep noted: "I could feel their urgency, an undercurrent of near panic . . . much needed to be organized and prepared."[21] As Miep and Jan stuffed clothing items into their coats and bags to take away, Miep noticed Edith's hair in disarray, and Anne's eyes "were like saucers, a mixture of excitement and terrible fright."[22]

No Time for Farewells

Anne felt sad that Hello and her girlfriends had to be left without a goodbye hug or a letter. It had to appear that the Franks had fled to Switzerland. Anne *did* take a phone call from Jacque late that Sunday, but was instructed by Edith not to breathe a word. Apparently Anne's acting skills fooled Jacque completely, for she had "no indication that she would disappear the following day."[23] Hello came by that Sunday evening, but was sent away. "I went home knowing somehow that I wouldn't see Anne again," he said. "These things happened . . . I was very disappointed, though."[24]

When told to pack her essential items into her schoolbag, Anne first packed her diary. She then selected her favorite books, curlers, comb and shawl, and old letters: "memories mean more to me than dresses," she wrote.[25] Grooming her thick, auburn hair was important, as well as keeping up on her reading. Most of her personal treasures had to be left behind.

Knowing that a Jewish family should never be seen carrying suitcases, Anne noted: "we put on heaps of clothes as if we were going to the North Pole."[26] In the light of a rainy dawn, braving the July heat, Margot Frank rode her bike off with Miep to open the hiding place. Soon after, Edith, Otto, and Anne followed on foot, lugging shopping bags and each still wearing the yellow star on his or her coat.

Hanne Goslar and Jacqueline van Maarsen went to the Franks to check on Anne. When Mr. Goldschmidt told them about the family's flight to Switzerland, Hanne and Jacque were amazed. Hanne decided Margot Frank had gotten an order to report to an *Arbeitslager*, or work camp. "We had no idea the family had been making preparations for a year," she said, noting that many Jews tried to escape over the Swiss border, but "most of them were not successful."[27] Jacque was shocked to see that Anne had left her new shoes, then spotted the new game Anne got for her birthday "which we had played like crazy the past few weeks, still lying there."[28]

Anne's First Days Inside the Annex

The hidden Annex consisted of three floors of spaces that backed onto the rear of the building, cut off and unused. Anne said: "No one would ever guess that there would be so many rooms hidden behind that plain door painted gray."[29] Otto had designed the spaces into a sleeping/reading room for himself and Edith, a shared room for Anne and Margot on the second floor, and a kitchen with pullout bed for the Van Pelses and a living area on the third floor. The only toilet was off this third floor living room. The Van Pelses' son Peter was relegated to a small hallway, leading to the front attic. The rooms were musty, suffocating with closed windows in the July heat, piled with supplies. Only when the company's workers had gone home, could the hidden residents venture downstairs. After realizing that these small plain rooms would be their home, possibly for years, Edith and Margot collapsed on their beds with headaches.

Anne followed Otto's lead, as he "hoped to quell his anxiety with well-organized activity."[30] Otto and Anne stitched pieces of fabric and hung them over the windows with thumbtacks. Blackout cardboards went up every night. As Anne unpacked, she found many household items that had disappeared from their home months ago. Anne discovered with delight her celebrity collection. Author Melissa Muller writes: "Mixed in with photos of . . . Greta Garbo and Ray Milland were innumerable pert, pudgy-cheeked offspring of European royal houses—the future Queen Elizabeth, for one."[31] With glue and ingenuity, Anne decorated the wall of her bedroom.

As the nearby Westerkerk clock chimed from its steeple, Anne wrote that the Annex suited her: "Although it leans to one side and is damp, you'd never find such a comfortable hiding place anywhere in Amsterdam."[32] Many Jews would hide in dark cellars and closets, freezing attics, and rat-infested barn lofts. Anne was correct about the Annex being a mansion in comparison.

Schedules were dictated by the hours of the workers downstairs and next door. Residents could make no noise during the day, not even to run the sink or flush the toilet.

This is how Otto Frank's office building at 263 Prinsengracht in Amsterdam looks today.

All waste had to be disposed of after hours. Only cold food, reading, naps and quiet activities filled the day. The active life of the family took place at night when the black screens covered the windows. The urge to speak or run up and down stairs got curtailed until after 6 P.M.

Friends Fill the Rooms

Anne awaited the arrival of the Van Pels family. "It will be much more fun and not so quiet. It is the silence that frightens me so . . . at night . . ."[33] The Van Pels family came a day early, for more call-ups had been sent out. Anne described Peter, whom she had known casually for years, as going on sixteen, shy, awkward, uninteresting. Peter's friendly cat lived in his cramped room or in the attic, where he would make his dinner from the rats. When Gusti van Pels opened her hatbox, it contained her personal chamber pot, for use when the toilet was off limits! The Franks were hungry for news. Many of their friends had been transported to Westerbork. People assumed the Franks had made it to Switzerland.

Getting the Annex into shape to accommodate seven people kept the Franks and the Van Pels busy most of July and August. Anne's limited sunbathing was managed by trips to the attic. Since no one outdoors could see through the roof window, it did not need to be curtained. Anne loved viewing the chestnut tree. It was all she would have to judge the passing of the seasons.

Otto told Anne, Margot, and Peter that he would tutor them in academic subjects, so they could return to the Jewish Lyceum caught up in their work. Anne wrote in her diary, "Daddy's the only one who understands me occasionally."[34] Her naturally exuberant, temperamental nature made Anne a challenge to live with. Now that she was trapped in small rooms night and day with her mother and sister, as well as the Van Pels family, friction was bound to happen. Edith felt she had to control Anne's restless behavior. Anne wrote that her mother either treated her "like a baby" or gave her "another frightful sermon."[35] Margot and Peter couldn't give enough help and comradeship to Anne, who felt isolated within herself.

Anne cheered when Miep came to pick up shopping lists and give bits of news. Miep's husband Jan ran up during his lunch hour. Bep visited when she could. Kleiman and Kugler consulted Otto and Hermann about business affairs and decisions. Miep returned at the end of the day to release them, announcing that all the workers had gone home, and they might sneak down to listen to the British broadcasts on the radio. Several times during the week, each of these saviors would deliver food and toiletries, purchased with hoarded ration books and money from the Franks and the Van Pels. Their visits were Anne's lifeline to the world, one in which she had lived a free, fun-filled life such a short time ago.

6

Life in the Annex

From the fall of 1942 throughout 1943, the Nazi's policy of transporting Jews out of Germany and the Netherlands to concentration camps was in full force. Since surrounding countries were either in Nazi hands or closing their borders to refugees, Jews had nowhere to emigrate. Anne was told by her parents that hiding in the Annex was their best hope of survival. She soon found out how difficult such a hidden life would be. At first, Margot was unable to be a close friend to Anne. Her way of coping was to be quiet, studious, undemanding. As Miep said of her: "Always kind, and always helpful, Margot had a way of making herself invisible."[1] Initially, Anne described Peter as lazy, doing a little carpentry work and secluding himself in his tiny bedroom.

Anne reported growing friction in her diary: quarrels between Mr. and Mrs. Van Pels (whom she called the Van Daans), arguments between Edith and Gusti. Anne noted that

Gusti had "taken all three of her sheets from out of the common linen cupboard, she takes it for granted that Mummy's sheets will do for all of us. It will be a nasty surprise for her when she finds that Mummy has followed her good example."[2] Anne admitted that Edith had hidden her good china and the family was using Gusti's, of which Anne had already broken several soup bowls.

Another conflict ignited over reading material. Johannes Kleiman brought books to the Annex each week, with varied subject matter. Peter got hold of a book about women, and "disappeared with his missive to the attic."[3] His father forbade the book, but Peter snuck it to his room, then forgot to return it before he got caught again. With a slap from his father, Peter lost his prize. Otto settled the fight, after which Peter went without dinner.

School Days Resume

Instructions began during September 1942, with Anne helping her father, nicknamed Pim by Anne and Margot, with Dutch lessons, Otto helping Anne with French, and all including Peter studying English. In addition to getting back into her studies, Anne was reading teen novels. While this improved Anne's mood, she still deeply missed her friends and going to school.

Miep found out that Jacque's family had been saved by her mother's clever deceptions. Only Jacque's father was Jewish; her mother, a French Catholic, had allowed her daughters to be accepted into the Jewish faith. Jacque's mother convinced the Nazi officials that Jacqueline and her older sister Christiane were really Christians, and she came up with baptismal certificates. "Jacque took off her Jewish star and switched from the Jewish lyceum to the highly regarded girls' lyceum . . . the right stamp in her identity papers had made

Hanneli Elizabeth "Hanne" Goslar

Born in Berlin in 1928, Hanneli (Hanne) fled with her family to Amsterdam in 1933. The Goslars were observant Orthodox Jews, and they became close friends with neighbors Otto and Edith Frank. Hanne gave Anne a deeper appreciation of Jewish holidays and Sabbath observance: "every Friday evening the Frank family came to visit us, and we also celebrated Passover together at our house."[4] The girls attended school together. They did homework together Sundays, and even spent summer holidays together. Hanne admired Anne's wit and sense of assurance: "my mother, who liked her very much, used to say, 'God knows everything, but Anne knows every-thing better.'"[5] Suddenly, the Franks vanished. The Goslars stayed, having bought passports from Paraguay. They had also been placed on a list of transports to Palestine. Then, Ruth Goslar died in childbirth, leaving Hanne to care for her two-year-old sister Gabriele.

After the Goslars were rounded up in June 1943, they were sent to Westerbork, the holding camp. The girls ended up in an orphanage. Although Gabi was ill, Hanne kept them going. In February 1944, they were sent to Bergen-Belsen. Through her own strength, faith, and determination to save her little sister, Hanne survived starvation and tuberculosis. After the war, she married, and became a nurse and citizen of Israel.

her an 'Aryan.'"[6] One by one, Anne's Ping-Pong pals Sanne Ledermann and Hanne Goslar and Ilse Wagner, and school chum Nanny Blitz were arrested and deported.

Bathing, Feeding, and Reading in the Annex

As the Annex had no plumbed bathtub, a washtub had to be filled with warmed water for each bath. Peter used the office kitchen, even though it had a glass door. Peter's father bathed in his own sleeping space. "Daddy has a bath in the private office, Mummy behind the fire guard in the kitchen, Margot and I have chosen the front office for our scrub."[7] The girls bathed on Saturday afternoons, when the curtains were drawn because the office was closed. After bathing, they peeked through a chink in the curtains, and gazed "in wonder at all the funny people outside."[8]

Miep and Jan Gies had to use contacts in the Dutch underground, called the National Relief Fund, to feed the seven hidden Jews. Everyone in the Annex gave Jan his or her identification cards, along with money. Jan used underground organizations to procure forged ration tickets, which he gave to Miep. By using these dangerous forgeries, Miep was able to buy food. Bep Voskuijl helped by getting extra milk. Hermann van Pels had a butcher friend who knew Miep was connected with the Van Pels family. This kindly butcher always gave her far more meat than she had tickets to buy. Jan's friend who owned a book shop and lending library gave Jan armloads each week without asking questions: "he was usually able to find what was desired, and for a few pennies he would borrow a pile of books."[9] Saturdays were book pickup and drop-off days. Anne and Margot retreated to the attic with their books, gaining some measure of precious privacy.

Stress Takes its Toll on Anne

In October, Anne wrote in her diary that Gusti van Pels had been attempting to flirt with Otto. "She strokes his face and hair, pulls her skirt right up and makes so-called witty remarks, trying in this way to attract Pim's attention." Although Otto never responded to Gusti's advances, Anne said she could not abide this behavior: "Mummy doesn't behave like that with Mr. v.P., I've said that to Mrs. v. P.'s face."[10]

Anne also got fed up with Margot being praised so much: "I keep teasing her all the time about being a model child which she can't stand, perhaps she'll give it up, it's high time."[11] Peter became more interesting to her. The two of them planned a skit for the family. "He appeared in one of Mrs. v. P.'s very narrow dress and I in his suit." With Peter in a woman's hat and Anne in a man's cap, their antics brought laughter to the rest of the residents.[12]

Being trapped with one's mother day and night in a small space would be difficult for most teenagers. Finally, Anne blew up at her mother in October and vented her anger to Kitty: "I simply can't stand Mummy, and I have to force myself not to snap at her all the time and to stay calm with her . . . I don't know how it is that I have taken such a terrible dislike to her."[13]

Another Desperate Friend Arrives

A friend of the Franks since 1938, Jewish dentist Fritz Pfeffer, and his Catholic girlfriend Charlotte "Lotte" Kaletta were members of the German immigrant group who met for socials at the Franks' Merwedeplein apartment.[14] Both previously divorced, Dr. Pfeffer and Lotte could not marry because of the Nuremberg Laws against gentiles marrying Jews. They were, however, a deeply committed couple. When the roundups of Jews became too dangerous in Amsterdam, Fritz had to go into hiding. Otto and Hermann could not refuse their frightened friend, so on November 16, 1942, Fritz moved into the Annex.[15] Lotte remained on the outside, where she struggled to get more ration cards and supplies for Fritz. Dr. Pfeffer, who was named Dr. Dussel in Anne's diary entries, smuggled in some dental equipment to care for the residents' teeth.

An appropriate place for Pfeffer to sleep was the issue. It was decided that Margot would sleep on a camp cot set up at the end of her parents' room, and Pfeffer would take her former bed in the small room with Anne. Since Anne was still considered a child, it would not be too immodest for them to share a room.

According to authors Ruud van der Rol and Rian Verhoeven, initially "Anne liked him, and listened to what he had to say about the outside world. It made everyone feel very somber."[16] Pfeffer explained that bounty hunters were rousting out Jews and collecting so much a head for turning them in.

Pfeffer had a teenage son from his first marriage, who had been sent to England to escape the war. Since he missed his son, he felt he had a parental duty to monitor Anne's behavior. He reported every infraction to Edith. Pfeffer was the loner among the eight, without the presence of his son or his beloved Lotte. Yet, Anne had no compassion for his situation. She quickly became as impatient with him as she was with the other adults.

December afternoons grew dark by four, but the workers below and on either side of the Annex did not all leave until six. This left almost two hours each day when the residents had to find silent activities to do in very low light. Due to so many hours of inactivity and not having regular physical exercise, Anne and the others experienced back and backside pains. Otto and Fritz devised exercise routines. Cleaning, cooking, scrubbing pots, and hand-washing all the laundry, then hauling it up to the attic to dry did keep the women fairly strong. Gusti became so excessive with exercises to control her weight, she fractured a rib.

Jewish and Christian Holidays Bring Pleasures

Anne reported to Kitty: "We didn't make much a fuss about Chanukah: we just gave each other a few trifles, and then we had the candle."[17] For conservation, they let the candles burn for only ten minutes. They sang the Chanukah songs in Hebrew. Using tools in the attic, Hermann van Pels made a *menorah*, or candle-holder, out of wood for the ceremony. In 1942, St. Nicholas Day fell immediately after Chanukah, so Miep, Bep, and the staff threw a surprise party for this Dutch day of celebration. The residents were given a large basket decorated with colored papers, a gift for each resident, and an appropriate poem to match. Delighted, Otto and Hermann gave little gifts to Miep and Bep left over from the good old days, as Anne put it, as well as some money. Anne enjoyed her Kewpie Doll. She reported that Bep's father, who worked as Hermann's replacement in the spice division, made a picture frame for Fritz, book ends for Otto, and an ashtray for Hermann.

Finding Space for Lessons

Hermann van Pels helped in the kitchen and created good sausages from scratch. Fritz Pfeffer, however, had little to do. "In the evening, he would often retire to the bathroom, where he could read in peace. During the day, he wanted to sit undisturbed at the little table in Anne's and his room, where he wrote and studied Spanish."[18] Now that it was cold and dark in the attic, Anne could not go upstairs much. She needed that table as well, to do her lessons and write in her diary. When Anne and Fritz fell to fighting over it, Otto worked out a table schedule. In an age when adult needs always ruled over the child's, Fritz as well as the Van Pelses considered Anne to be terribly indulged. Yet Otto knew Anne well; to repress her would bring on severe depression.

That winter the three teens studied languages, history, geography, and religious history. A correspondence course in stenography was sent to the office, from which Anne and Margot learned shorthand in several languages. "Bep Voskuijl sent Margot's shorthand exercises in under her own name," and "they came back with high grades."[19] Anne's favorite subject continued to be history, especially Greek and Roman mythology. Otto forced her to continue math, and if she lagged, he punished her: "Daddy is grumbling again, and threatens to take my diary away, oh insuperable horror."[20] She vowed to hide it if he tried.

Since the original red plaid diary was now filled to capacity, Anne had to use notebooks brought to her by Miep to continue her entries. She made reference to journals that Margot was keeping as well. Otto brought up an index card file and required the teens to note the books they read with author and date. They also were to expand their vocabulary.

During night air raids, Anne admitted that she often crawled into bed with Otto for comfort. Anne knew she was acting childish, but told Kitty that the antiaircraft guns made so much noise she could hardly hear herself speak. It was not her Pim that comforted Anne one night. Scared of the dark, she begged Otto to relight the candle during bursts of gunfire. He refused. Edith could not bear Anne's terror, relit the

candle, and told Otto that Anne was not a soldier! After this, Anne wrote that she would try harder to love her mother.

The Führer's War Broadens

The Nazi armed forces directed their efforts in 1943 to combating Allied air attacks on Germany, holding off the Soviet forces in battles on the eastern front, and waging the battle of the Atlantic. During this campaign, American and British ships and submarines fought the German navy. German and Italian forces in Tunisia failed against British and United States troops.[21]

Nazi forces were systematically destroying Poland's Jewish population. A half million Jews had been herded into a large ghetto in Warsaw. By the end of 1942, there were only seventy thousand of them left alive. The rest had been taken to camps like Treblinka to be killed. In April 1943, a stalwart group staged a ghetto uprising against the Nazis. For a shining moment, these Jews held off overwhelming forces. Eventually, the Nazi army regrouped and blew up the ghetto.

Illness Increases Everyone's Anxiety

In April, the health of the residents of the Annex and their supporters deteriorated. Anne suffered rages, spells of weeping, and pounding headaches. Historian Carol Ann Lee noted that Anne took valerian pills every day. Valerian is a common herb used to combat depression.[22] To make matters

Anne glimpsed this clock tower, called Westerclerk, through her attic window and heard it chime each quarter-hour.

worse, Anne discovered she had outgrown everything. Miep promised to buy whatever dresses and slippers she could on the black market.

Hermann van Pels, usually an amusement to Anne with his jokes and horsing around, caught a cold and treated himself endlessly with chamomile tea and Mentholatum. Bep came down with the flu. Kleiman, "the one who always cheers us up, has got a hemorrhage of the stomach" Anne reported, and "Mr. Voskuijl is going to the Hospital next week. He has probably got an abdominal ulcer."[23]

In May, Anne pleased Edith by shampooing and combing out her hair. "We have to make do with sticky green soap," she explained, as the shampoo was long gone, and "the family comb has got a mere 10 teeth."[24] Anne noted that the quality of food had gotten boring and disgusting; she quipped that if you were trying to diet, the Annex was a good place to live.

Anne's fourteenth birthday was celebrated on June 13, 1943. Otto wrote her birthday poem in German, which Margot translated into Dutch. This delighted Anne, who found it both accurate and amusing. Otto's gentle verses rang true:

> Please bear with us, your parents, for we try To judge you fairly and with sympathy. Correction sometimes take against your will, Though it's like swallowing a bitter pill; Which must be done if we're to keep the peace, While time goes by till all this suffering cease.[25]

Otto went on to joke about the fact that Anne had outgrown her clothes. This made Anne smile. The gifts everyone showered her with made Anne feel completely spoiled during such austere times, especially the sweets and a huge book on her favorite subject of mythology.

Anne Begins Her Creative Writing

Anne composed essays during the summer of 1943, and then added short stories. Her wit and sense of humor never failed her, even when recounting a personal assault by Mouschi's fleas, and the potato-peeling battle between Hermann, Gusti, and Edith over division of labor between girls vs. boys, with Fritz trying to mediate. Anne's conclusion: "If Father weren't much too good to such people, he could remind them that we and the others literally saved their lives. In a labor camp, they'd have to do worse things than peel potatoes . . . or even hunt cat fleas."[26] Anne's work was written each day with amazing precision, in ink, with very few crossed out words or corrections, in complete sentence structure.[27]

A Threat of Discovery!

Everyone feared that burglars would break in and discover signs of hidden Jews. After an unsuccessful break-in on the exterior doors before July 16, a true burglary occurred. All the residents slept through it. When Peter went down at 7 A.M. for his regular checkup on the doors and warehouse, he discovered the warehouse door and the street door had both been opened. He raced to tell Otto, who searched for anything amiss, and turned the radio to a German station. It had been set on the British station, a dead giveaway. Kleiman reported that the burglars "stole 2 cash boxes . . . postal orders and checkbooks, and then worst of all, all our sugar coupons."[28] After the terror of possibly being discovered passed, everyone was so relieved that they hardly noticed an anniversary. They were in hiding for one year.

Anne noted that all of the Annex residents shared a fantasy of freedom. She asked what each person would like *first* upon liberation? Both Margot and Hermann told her they dreamed of a hot bathtub filled to the brim for a long soak. Gusti wanted a lovely cake. She recorded that Pfeffer "thinks of nothing but seeing his Charlotte; Mummy, her cup of coffee." Peter longed to stroll through the downtown, and Otto wanted to visit his sick friend Mr. Voskuijl. Anne burst out: "I long for a home of our own, to be able to move around freely . . . in other words—back to school!"[29]

7

The Young Writer

To give her life in hiding some excitement, Anne wrote about the smallest incidents. During 1943, every hour was programmed for each resident, lest they give themselves away by light, smells, or sounds. Anne made witty reports of everyone's activities, including the trials of toilet use, with chamber pots required during "no-flush hours," and the one toilet often being used by Dr. Pfeffer. She was pleased to see her father progressing with his English, seated on his sagging, squeaky bed, reading the novels of Charles Dickens with his dictionary beside him. She marveled at all her mother accomplished in terms of handiwork, reading, and family management. According to historian Carol Ann Lee, Anne enjoyed evenings when "they listened to classical music on the radio, played board games, recited poetry, and discussed politics."[1] Otto taught his daughters about the great German writers, and read aloud from Heine, Goethe, and Schiller.

Lee says that each Friday evening "they observed the Sabbath, led by Edith Frank and Fritz Pfeffer."[2] Anne indicated that before bed, she said prayers as her father listened.

A fright occurred when the owner of 263 Prinsengracht abruptly sold the building. Historian Ernst Schnabel says that when the buyers came to inspect the property, Victor Kugler "showed them the storerooms and offices, but told them he could not take them to the rear of the building because he had unfortunately mislaid the key. There were a few more rooms there, he said, but nothing in particular to see." Amazingly, the buyers left, satisfied, and apparently never returned to the building.[3]

Anne Begins her Creative Writing

Miep and Bep gave Margot and Anne office work to help keep the business running. The girls became very good at making bookkeeping entries and filing letters. Peter performed duties from the attic to warehouse. In spite of attempts to keep busy and organized, stress affected everyone. Anne remarked to Kitty: "A good hearty laugh would help more than 10 valerian pills, but we've almost forgotten how to laugh . . . Everyone here looks with fear and misgivings toward that great terror, winter."[4]

Anne used what she could see of humanity through the small opening in the drapes, and her vivid imagination, to create tales of life in the world. During that summer, according to the United States Holocaust Memorial Museum, "Anne began to write stories, fairy tales, and essays, . . . On September 2, she began to copy them into a notebook, added a table of contents to resemble a published book, and gave it the title *Stories and Events from the Annex*." She intended to submit a fairy tale to a Dutch magazine.[5] In her sketch called "Kitty," August 1943, she envisioned the family life of a poor girl next door. Kitty comforts her mother who weeps from exhaustion in the night; she longs to grow up and earn money. "Kitty's mother always says that a girl doesn't get a husband if she is too clever, and that, Kitty thinks, would be just awful. Later she should like to have dear little children, but not such children as her brothers and sisters. Kitty's children are going to be much prettier and sweeter."[6] One wonders if Anne ever heard Edith weep during these nights, or if Anne had been told she was too clever for her own good. Whatever truth lay in the tales, Anne avidly wrote them.

The Van Pelses Run Short of Cash

The financial burden of paying for all their food and supplies had been split proportionately between Otto, Hermann, and Fritz. Tension grew as the Van Pelses' finances were depleting, and Hermann got caught hoarding some food. To raise money, Anne noted, Gusti "will certainly have to part with her fur coat. . . . They've had a terrific row upstairs about it."[7] Screaming and swearing at each other and then reconciling was routine for the Van Pelses. Anne noticed "Daddy goes about with his lips tightly pursed," knowing he is the eternal peacemaker.[8] Edith wore a blotched red face, Margot came down with headaches, and Pfeffer couldn't sleep. Anne said "I sometimes forget who we are quarreling with."[9]

Darker Daydreams Worry Anne

Although Anne enthusiastically worked on her studies, and admired her father and sister who were learning Latin through a correspondence course, her daydreams grew darker. To Anne, the concept of a postwar world was like "only a castle in the air, something that will never really happen."[10] She described a surreal image of being surrounded by danger, trapped by impenetrable dark clouds threatening to crush them. When her wit returned, she composed in comic tones an "Ode to My Fountain Pen," her beloved gift from Grandmother Frank, which somehow fell into the stove and got burned.

Anne wrote in November 1943 of a vision she had of Hanneli Goslar, thin, in rags, with fear in her eyes, crying: "Oh Anne, why have you deserted me? Help me, help me, rescue me from this hell!" Although Anne is helpless to save Hanneli, she prays to God to spare her friend. "Why should I be chosen to live and she probably to die?. . . Why are we so far from each other now?"[11] Hanneli, her little sister Gabi and her father had been rounded up the previous June, and put into Westerbork. The Goslar girls were in good condition, and would be transported to Bergen-Belsen the following February, where they were allowed to stay together as a family and work.[12]

European Resistance Brings Hope

Otto Frank and the other Annex residents closely followed Europe's resistance of the Nazis. The French had been split between territory occupied by the Nazis, and territory which remained Free France. The *Conseil National de la Resistance*, which included non-communist French Resistance groups, met in Paris.[13] These freedom fighters gave their support to General Charles de Gaulle, whose force was based in Algiers, with management of the nation's interests. De Gaulle remained President of France throughout the war and headed its resistance. In Yugoslavia, resistance partisans got a boost after Italy surrendered to the armies of U.S. Army General Dwight Eisenhower and British Field Marshal Bernard Montgomery. British Prime Minister Winston Churchill asked his agents to find out who was killing the most Nazis in Yugoslavia.

When he was told it was partisan leader Josip Broz Tito, he put Britain's forces behind him. President Franklin Roosevelt followed suit. Tito's armies fought the Nazis continually throughout 1943.[14]

The U.S. Air Force bombed Germany, specifically targeting Berlin, Leipzig, and Frankfurt.[15] Although many planes were shot down by German antiaircraft fire, the damage to German war industries was substantial. The war in the Soviet Union went back and forth, with Germany taking hard losses. Still, Hitler's armed forces held their conquered nations under military rule. The Annex residents longed to hear General Eisenhower's voice on BBC (British radio), announcing an Allied land invasion of Europe.

Miep Helps Keep Anne Dressed

Although severe shortages afflicted the Dutch, Mrs. Kleiman tried to get extra used clothing for Anne on the pretext of dressing her own daughter. Miep Gies grew close to Anne, since she understood "how much pretty things meant to young ladies of fourteen, who were just beginning to feel pretty themselves."[16] Miep came across a pair of second-hand but good red leather high heels. As Anne paraded in them, Miep thought she had never seen anyone so happy.

Miep herself had a secret at this time, one she found out in the fall of 1943. Her husband Jan had joined a Resistance group. Miep never told the Franks, but supported Jan. "As a fellow resister, I was happy that he'd found a new way to go against our oppressors."[17]

With the December 1943 holidays coming, Anne devised a celebration. This year, they had no money to buy gifts on the black market, and few treasures left from their old life. The Van Pelses sold Gusti's coats and jewelry on the black market for food money. All Anne and Otto had to use was

Dwight David Eisenhower

Born in 1890 and raised in Abilene, Kansas, Dwight Eisenhower, also known as Ike, was a determined student. A classmate at Abilene High said: "I never heard him say 'I don't know.'"[18] A dedicated cadet at West Point, he later served in World War I, commanding a tank brigade, and won the Distinguished Service Medal. Eisenhower worked his way up in rank, and by June 1928, graduated from the War College. He was first in his class.[19]

After serving as aide to Chief of Staff General Douglas MacArthur in the Phillipines, Eisenhower was promoted again. War in Europe thrust him into a major role to "help prepare the American Army to fight the Wehrmacht [German Army].[20] He told his boss General George Marshall that the United States needed to "crack Germany through England . . . we've got to build up air and land forces in England and when we're strong enough, go after Germany's vitals."[21] His plan, Operation Overlord, directed U.S. and British divisions to assault the coast of occupied France in early summer 1944. Eisenhower made the D-day invasion work on June 6, 1944. His forces liberated France and fought through to Berlin. After being Chief of Staff under President Harry Truman, Dwight D. Eisenhower became President of the United States in 1952.

their sense of humor, so they wrote each person a verse. Quietly on St. Nicholas eve, Anne and Otto stole a shoe from each resident, placed a poem in each, and loaded a decorated laundry basket with this wit-filled footwear. They wrote a poem for the whole group which ended:

> Still we'll make his spirit live
> And since we've nothing left to give
> We've thought of something else to do
> . . .
> Each please look inside his shoe.[22]

Shortly after, Anne fell ill with the flu. Every home remedy known in 1943 was given her, for the sound of coughing could put the Annex residents in danger of being heard. Fritz Pfeffer tried to use his medical knowledge to speed Anne's recovery but only succeeded in embarrassing her. She complained to Kitty: "Why should this fellow come and lie [his head] on my heart? He's not my lover after all!"[23]

The Chanukah and Christmas season brought restored health to Anne, and peace to the house. Anne used her hoarded sugar allotment to make "little creamy confections" for Miep, who said "Anne made me taste them right away, in order to watch the look on my face. She laughed, her eyes glistening, as I licked my fingers."[24]

Dreaming of a career in Hollywood, Anne wrote a fantasy about this subject: "I was seventeen, an attractive girl with flirtation eyes and a wealth of dark curls—a teenager filled with ideals, illusions and daydreams. In one way or another, the day would come when my name would be a household word . . . "[25] The tale casts Anne as a penpal of American film performer Priscilla Lane and her sisters, who invite her to be their guest in Hollywood. There Anne gets a modeling job, and finds out how hard models and film stars work for their living.

Anne Assesses Her Feelings

As 1943 came to an end, Anne faced her conflicted emotions about being forced into hiding. Mrs. Kleiman's visits were welcomed, but stories of her daughter's clubs, school plays, and parties made Anne deeply jealous. Although Anne knew she was fortunate compared to other Jewish children, a year and a half of captivity and repression had taken a toll. "Cycling, dancing, whistling, looking out at the world, feeling young, to know that I'm free—that's what I long for; still I mustn't show it." She wondered if anyone could forget she is Jewish and just let her be "a young girl in me who is badly in need of some rollicking fun."[26]

To celebrate New Year's Day, Miep and Jan held a party for the residents. They brought black-market beer, and special baked goods. Miep baked Anne's favorite spice cake and wrote with frosting on top: "PEACE 1944!" Jan Gies enthralled Anne with stories of Resistance fighters and acts of sabotage, yet never revealed that he was part of the underground.

During the early winter of 1944, the Franks, the Van Pelses, and Dr. Pfeffer lived on a poor, dwindling food supply and endured frayed clothing and increasingly difficult laundry and hygiene problems. During her year and a half in hiding, Anne filled up her original diary and at least one other notebook with her entries. Many of them centered on venting her anger on Edith. After a year and a half, Anne realized that she had been very hard on her mother, probably due to her own issues with puberty and entering womanhood. Her physical changes, Anne told Kitty, were of absorbing interest to her. "Each time I have a period, (and that has only been three times) I have the feeling that in spite of all the pain, unpleasantness, and nastiness I have a sweet secret."[27] She longed for her friends but realized she only had Margot, whom she loved but with whom she hadn't been that close, and Peter van Pels.

Given their mutual loneliness, the two sisters became better friends. In February, Margot turned eighteen. One morning that month Anne and Margot had "a fit of 'helpless laughter,' you know, the sort we used to have at school. Margot and I were giggling like real schoolgirls."[28] Margot started treating Anne more like an equal, which Anne greatly appreciated. They even wrote each other letters, sharing their feelings.

Anne never stopped caring about her personal grooming. "She manicured her nails, tried to bleach her [upper lip] with peroxide," noted historian Melissa Muller.[29] In January, Anne remarked in her diary that she was trying new hair styles, even though the adults teased her about trying to look like her favorite film stars. Peter van Pels had to notice, as they were thrown together constantly.

Peter had also matured over the year and a half in hiding, from a petulant boy to a more responsible young man with many jobs in the annex and office. Like Anne, he must have been desperately in need of some emotional and physical contact. By the winter of 1944, Anne was ready. She started finding times to come to Peter's space and talk to him.

Gusti's Gift

In February, after Margot's birthday, Miep Gies turned thirty-five. Miep expected nothing but hugs. However, Gusti van Pels took her aside and said: "Herman and I have been wanting to find a way to express the inexpressible. But there are no words. This is just a small token of our appreciation and friendship."[30] Gusti had not sold her antique onyx and diamond ring, which she presented to Miep. Knowing how hungry Hermann was for sausages and cigarettes, Miep

realized that the need to show his respect for her sacrifice ran even deeper. She promised to wear the ring forever.

Anne's Tales Explore her Fantasies

Anne wrote a sketch that month she called *The Flower Girl*, about Krista, a girl of twelve who lived with her older sister. In the story, Krista survived through a long hard day of gathering, preparing, and selling flowers. Her backbreaking day ended at sunset. Anne wrote:

> . . . nobody need think the hardworking little flower girl is dissatisfied . . . in the field, amid the flowers, beneath the darkening sky, Krista is content. Gone is the fatigue, gone is the market, gone are the people. The little girl dreams and thinks only of the bliss of having, each day, this short while alone with God and nature.[31]

How suffocated Anne must have felt at that time. When Miep or Bep came in straight off the wintry streets, Anne would press her face against their coats to inhale the fresh air of freedom.

Many Dutch non-Jews, according to Jan Gies and Johannes Kleiman, had also gone underground or into hiding to avoid being conscripted or forced into hard labor at foreign factories. Anne marveled at the courage of the Dutch Resistance workers, and noted: "Our helpers are a very good example, they have pulled us through up till now and we hope they will bring us safely to dry land . . . never have we heard one word of the burden which we certainly must be." She observed

Visitors to the Anne Frank House can see the Annex entrance, which is hidden by a bookcase.

that while others proved courageous in battle against the Germans, their helpers showed their heroism every day by bringing them supplies, good spirits, and affection in the face of danger.[32]

Anne and Margot Reveal their Feelings

By mid-March, Anne and Peter had grown close, sharing everything two teenagers could possibly discuss. Anne's worry was that Margot liked Peter in the same way and was being cut out. Margot confessed her deeper feelings to her sister in a letter, which Anne called "evidence of Margot's goodness."[33]

Margot wrote: "Anne, when I said yesterday that I was not jealous of you, I was only fifty percent honest . . . I'm jealous of neither you nor Peter. I only feel . . . a bit sorry that I haven't found anyone yet, and am not likely to for the time being, with whom I can discuss my thoughts and feelings."[34]

She assured Anne that she was not taking something Margot felt entitled to, and that since they were already missing out on so much of life, she hoped Anne and Peter could put their trust completely in each other. Anne, very touched by her sister's feelings, urged her to keep writing. Anne assured Margot: "You don't know how much I admire you, and I only hope that I may yet acquire some of the goodness that you and Daddy have, because now I don't see much difference in that sense."[35] Anne preserved Margot's letters by keeping them in her diary.

Anne Grows in Many Ways

In spite of food shortages, Anne continued to develop. People who supplied Jan and Miep with black market food coupons got arrested, Miep and Bep caught the flu, and Kleiman's stomach ulcers flared up. This left the residents dining on a typical lunch of mashed potatoes and pickled kale, which Anne could barely swallow. Still, she grew five inches from July 1942 when she entered the Annex, until spring of 1944.[36] Being stuck in close quarters for almost two years with unhappy adults and having to sleep with the snoring Fritz Pfeffer was becoming truly awkward for a girl past puberty. However, she enjoyed her time with Peter.

8

A Threat Outside the Door

Anne and Peter often went to the attic after evening chores during March, to breathe in the night air and star gaze through the high window. They found they could openly discuss every subject, including sex, contraception, and "how boys could tell they are grown up."[1] Peter became Anne's favorite confidant. She even told him about her plan to become a writer in her adult life. She later told Kitty: "I want to go on living even after my death! And therefore I am grateful to God for giving me this gift . . . of expressing all that is in me."[2] Anne confessed to Kitty that she was like someone in love who could only talk about her darling. When would she and Peter reveal a budding love affair? ". . . sooner than I think! I get an understanding look from him about twice a day, I wink back, and we both feel happy."[3] Soon Anne was living for her meetings with Peter.

A Complicated Burglary Confuses Everyone

On March 1, 1944, Anne reported that burglars again struck their offices. In the evening Hermann van Pels went down to the offices below. "He saw that the communicating glass door and the office door were open," with a mess in the main office, and "to satisfy himself he went straight downstairs, took hold of the front door, felt the yale lock and found everything closed." Hermann said nothing. When Peter went down the next morning, he found the front door wide open! Apparently the thief had a copy of the master key to the building, and fled with his stolen goods after Hermann left.[4]

The Dutch are Prompted to Save their Diaries

The Dutch minister for education, art, and science spoke on the BBC at the end of March. When he urged the Dutch "to preserve their diaries, letters, and documents to show later 'what we as a nation have had to endure and overcome during these years,' Anne began to rewrite her diary with a view to publication."[5] She revised from the journal's beginning up to the present month, March 1944. The curators of the United States Holocaust Memorial Museum, in a booklet on Anne as a writer, stated:

> Hoping to publish it after the war under the title *The Secret Annex* . . . she transferred nearly two-thirds of her diary from her original notebooks to loose sheets of paper, making various revisions. Anne rearranged or combined entries, shortened or expanded them, and invented pen names for the inhabitants of the Annex.[6]

As Anne locked her writings in Otto's briefcase, she mused: "it would be quite funny 10 years after the war if people were told how we Jews lived and what we ate and talked about here."[7]

Radio Orange BBC kept everyone updated on air-raid announcements and war news. Anne noted that the newscaster "Frank Phillips or Her Majesty Queen Wilhelmina. . . . each get their turn and an ever attentive ear, and if they [the adults] are not eating or sleeping, then they are sitting around the radio and discussing food, sleep and politics."[8] Bombings were frequent and close enough that Anne said the houses around them trembled like blades of grass in the wind.

Anne noted on March 31: "Hungary is occupied by German troops. There are still 1 million Jews there, so they too will have had it now!"[9] Her grasp of the political situation was growing more astute by necessity. Historian Michael Marrus states: "In May 1944 the deportations of Hungarian Jewry to Auschwitz began, carrying over 400,000 Jews northward to their deaths."[10] The massive concentration camp of Auschwitz was located near Krakow, Poland.

Those Dreaded Food Cycles

In April, Anne groaned to Kitty about "food cycles," long periods when the residents were fed nothing but one or two foods. Endive, turnips, kidney beans, and even sauerkraut were bought when large quantities became available, and had to be spread over every meal. "I must tell you about the dumplings, which we make out of government flour, water and yeast. They are so sticky and tough, they lie like stones in one's stomach," Anne complained, and then admitted: "But we are still alive and even enjoy things quite often!"[11]

A Major Break-in Threatens All

On Easter Sunday, April 9, 1944, Peter warned the older men that during his evening inspection he heard burglars. The men rushed down to inspect the situation. The women stayed upstairs, hearing a number of loud bangs. When the men

When Anne peeked through the curtains at Otto's front office window, she saw traffic and houseboats on the Prinsengracht—just as one could see in May 2004.

returned, Anne dramatized the incidents. The thieves had bashed a large hole in the front door and were in the act of entering. Hermann, instinctively, shouted: "Police!" Twice the burglars fled, then returned, until Anne said: "Now we are lost!"

The next day, Easter Monday, was a Dutch work holiday, so no workers were expected at the offices. Otto managed a phone call to Kugler, who warned Miep and Jan Gies. Miep and Jan hurried over, seeing the broken door and mess inside. "Anne ran and threw her arms around my neck," Miep said; "She was in tears."[12] The residents were still paralyzed with fear, afraid even to use the toilet.

After Jan repaired the door, he ordered the men: "Stay behind the bookcase, no matter what. If you hear something, never go. Be silent, wait. Never go."[13] Ashamed, Otto and the men admitted they had acted badly. Not only did the lives of the eight in hiding depend on secrecy, but the lives of the employees and others who helped them were also in jeopardy. Later, Anne marveled that they had been spared: "God truly protected us, just think of it—the police at our secret cupboard, the light on right in front of it, and still we remained undiscovered."[14]

The next week, Miep went to the grocer who had always sold them more potatoes and vegetables than she and Jan had rations for, and discovered he'd been arrested—for hiding two Jews in his own home. Miep said: "The arrest of this man was a major catastrophe. Because he'd been so kind, I'd been able to keep feeding all eight in hiding."[15] Determined and inventive, Miep cultivated friendship with another food supplier and kept the residents from starving.

Anne Creates a World of Tales and Romance

In spite of the threatening events, Anne kept up her spirits while writing. She produced tales about Dora the elf, an ancient dwarf, a bear called Blurry, an Angora cat named Muriel, and Ellen the Fairy, which she liked to read aloud. They contrasted with her darker essays, which questioned social injustice. Her romantic relationship with Peter progressed, and she received her first kiss. She wondered if her parents would approve "of my sitting and kissing a boy on a divan—a boy of seventeen and half and a girl of just under fifteen? I don't really think they would, but I must rely on myself over this. It is so quiet and peaceful to lie in his arms and to dream."[16] As the spring weather grew warm, Bep brought narcissus and grape hyacinth, and the chestnut tree beyond the attic window bloomed. Anne said she felt hope rise in her heart.

How the Jews were Surviving

What Anne and her family could not know is that over 3,370 Dutch gentiles were aiding Jews in escaping or hiding. Many Jews were hidden in monasteries or churches, or in rural villages and farms. Some of the Dutch rescuers' motives were not laudable. For example, some took payment from their hidden Jews or they used them for free farm labor. Most of the Dutch motives were loftier, such as a hatred of the Nazi occupiers, and strong religious belief that the Jews did not deserve to be punished or deported.

The Dutch nickname for people in hiding was *onderduikers*, meaning people who dove under. A larger formal group called the National Organization for Assistance to Divers was founded in 1942 by a housewife and a Christian minister.[17] It is unclear whether this group helped Jan Gies get the stolen or counterfeited ration coupons needed to keep the eight Annex divers alive. Another underground worker was Leesha Bos, a teenager no older than Margot Frank, who was a nurse in Haarlem. She was recruited as a courier to *onderduikers*, and became the lifeline for hidden people, who awaited her every visit. "Very often I was the only outside person whom they saw in their isolation," Leesha said:

> I brought them news and stories from the outside. I supplied them with food ration cards . . . I was shocked to see the pitiful condition of most of the people in hiding. The starvation diet of less than five-hundred calories a day had left them skinny, weak, and without resistance to sickness.[18]

Eva Geiringer

Anne and Margot's friends from Merwedeplein, Eva and Heinz Geiringer, led a pleasant life as students until Heinz got his call-up notice the same day as Margot. Eva and her mother Elfriede hurried to their appointed hiding place, hardly having time to kiss Erich and Heinz goodbye as they left for theirs.

While in hiding, Eva's mother taught her lessons. "I struggled along on my own, missing the company of other pupils intensely," Eva said.[19] Weekend reunions with her father and brother were possible. "Since we were both fair skinned and looked like any other Dutch mother and daughter, with luck we could walk incognito in the crowd."[20] On Eva's fifteenth birthday in May 1944, the Gestapo hauled them to headquarters, where Erich and Heinz waited. Erich promised the Nazis valuable jewels if they would not send the family who hid them to prison. "The Germans need not have kept their word . . . but they did," Eva said.[21]

Eva and her family were eventually sent to Auschwitz/Birkenau. Eva contracted typhus, but she recovered. Eva endured through malnutrition, filth, and frostbite. In January 1945, Birkenau was liberated. Eva's mother Elfriede survived with her, but her father and brother died. Eva said about 18-year-old Heinz: "He was a talented boy . . . his young life was terminated without any reason."[22]

Although Leesha had Jewish parents, she was able to obtain false Aryan identification papers, and continued her work throughout the war.

Adversity Gives Anne Strength

The food supplies in the Annex deteriorated in May 1944, with only two meals being served a day. Anne noted wryly: "Vegetables are still very difficult to get hold of, we had rotten boiled lettuce this afternoon . . . with these we eat rotten potatoes, so it's a delicious combination!"[23] The serious lack of nutrition took its toll on everyone's bodies and minds. Anne often asked herself why people did not live peacefully together, but then observed that not just the politicians and capitalists were guilty of the war. There was in all people "simply an urge to destroy, an urge to kill, to murder and rage . . ."[24] Yet from her misery, Anne felt she had gained emotional strength. "I have now reached the stage that I can live entirely on my own, without Mummy's support or anyone else's . . . it's been a bitter, hard struggle . . . now the battle is over. I have won! I am independent both in mind and body."[25]

Will Liberation Ever Come?

The Dutch royal family, still in exile in England, kept up their broadcasts on Radio Orange BBC. Queen Wilhelmina on May 11 urged the Dutch to await her return to the Netherlands, and encouraged their heroic behavior. The Dutch were eagerly awaiting the Allied landing in occupied Europe. On May 13, 1944, Otto Frank celebrated his fifty-fifth birthday and his nineteenth wedding anniversary with Edith. Miep and Bep outdid themselves on the black market, providing gifts for the Van Pelses, Pfeffer, and the others to give him. "He was certainly spoiled," Anne wrote happily. "Fifty fancy pastries arrived from Siemons, heavenly! Daddy also treated us to spiced gingerbread, beer for the gentlemen and yoghourt for the ladies. Enjoyment all around!"[26]

By May 22, Otto lost a bet of five bottles of yogurt with Gusti that the invasion would have happened by then. Anne estimated that the entire population of western Europe talked of nothing but liberation by the Allies. A frightening possibility was also being discussed: Anne heard that German Jews who moved to the Netherlands due to Nazi persecution might not keep "the right of asylum in Holland but when Hitler is gone they will have to go back to Germany again . . . I love Holland. I who, having no native country, had hoped that it would become my fatherland, and I still hope it will!"[27]

Invasion at Last!

Invasion of the west coast of France by Allied forces began on June 5 with the Allied ships sailing the channel. On that day in Italy, "the Allied forces made their triumphal entry into Rome and push(ed) on beyond in pursuit of the retreating Germans."[28] With tidal conditions ideal, the Allies planned to land units of four army corps and three airborne divisions on the beaches of Normandy, France under the command of the Supreme Allied Commander in Europe, General Dwight D. Eisenhower. On June 6, 1944, this huge military operation landed at Normandy. German General Irwin Rommel made sure his forces put up heavy resistance, and fighting was fierce on all fronts. The United States troops who landed at Caen suffered the most casualties. Allied air support helped the ground forces to succeed.

As Miep Gies rode her bicycle to the office on the Prinsengracht, she felt "a buzz in the air, like electricity. People were animated as they hadn't been in years."[29]

A new warehouse foreman had been hired after Bep Voskuijl's father became too ill with cancer to continue. Willem van Maaren was a good worker, but not trustworthy enough to share in the secret of the hiders. Once, Van Maaren was caught by Victor Kugler looking up through a scratched opening in a painted-over window, towards the upstairs Annex. Kugler noted: "Van Maaren had noticed that the office and storerooms were used at night, and he concluded that whoever was poking around there in the dark must be hiding in the Annex during the day."[30] Kugler found him spreading potato flour to pick up footprints and putting pencils where anyone moving in the night could knock them off. He then learned that Van Maaren was sheltering his adult son, who was avoiding forced labor service in Germany. Because of this, Van Maaren wanted no trouble from the Nazi police over hiders in his workplace.

Anne Maintains Her Ideals

"My birthday has gone by again, so now I'm fifteen," Anne wrote to Kitty on June 13, 1944. She received much needed underwear, books on the history of art, and on botany, a double bracelet from Margot, quite a few sweet treats from the others. Miep and Bep found blank lined books for Anne to continue writing her diary entries and stories.[31] Miep said that Peter gave her a few precious coins and asked her to buy the nicest flowers she could find. "A lovely bunch of peonies from Peter" pleased Anne greatly. Then Anne included the war news: "Yesterday Churchill, Smutz, Eisenhower and Arnold visited French villages which have been conquered and liberated. The torpedo boat that Churchill was in shelled the coast, he appears, like so many men, not to know what fear is; makes me envious!"[32]

105

The summer was filled with hope for everyone in the Annex that they would survive in hiding long enough to see the Allies liberate the Netherlands. On July 15, Anne wrote a lengthy entry, marking the two years that she and the others had been in hiding. After a thoughtful assessment of what her life had been trapped in the Annex, Anne wrote:

> It's really a wonder that I haven't dropped all my ideals, because they seem so absurd and impossible to carry out. Yet I keep them, because in spite of everything I still believe that people are really good at heart. . . . I see the world gradually being turned into a wilderness, I hear the ever approaching thunder, which will destroy us too, I can feel the sufferings of millions and yet, if I look up into the heavens, I think that . . . this cruelty too will end, and that peace and tranquility will return again.[33]

Betrayed!

On the first of August, Anne wrote an entry, which tried to examine the good and bad sides of her personality. As always, she locked her diary entries into Otto's briefcase. On the morning of August 4, 1944, the offices of Opetka were operating, Otto was giving Peter an English lesson, and the others were about their morning chores. As Kleiman, Miep, and Bep worked in the front office, a man in civilian clothes, holding a revolver, marched in and ordered them all to stay put. He went to the rear office where Kugler worked, leaving Miep and Bep trembling in fear.

Miep later said that as soon as the armed man left, she "took the illegal ration cards, the money, and (Jan's) lunch out of my bag . . . after a very short time I heard the familiar sound of Henk's footsteps on the stairs." Miep ran to stop her husband, saying it had gone wrong there. He understood instantly and whisked the incriminating things away. Bep started crying.

Kleiman told her to run to the drugstore and "telephone my wife and tell her what has happened and then disappear."[34] He then told Miep Gies to run as well—but Miep noted later that she wouldn't leave.

Kugler was forced to reveal the eight residents. With guns pointed, the Dutch Nazi Green Police ordered them to leave with hands raised. Otto said that after taking his cashbox, the policeman reached for his brief case: "He shook everything out, dumped the contents on the floor, so that Anne's papers and notebooks and loose sheets lay scattered all over the floorboards. Then he put our valuables into the brief case. . . ."[35] The residents who held onto hope for over two years in hiding left with dignity. Anne Frank's diary, notebooks, and lesson books lay in the dust.

9

Anne in Prison

The Annex residents were detained at an old school building, now Gestapo headquarters. Eva Geiringer, who was detained there in May, described it: "There were soldiers everywhere . . . rooms for documentation, and cells too. They wanted us to give them information on those who had protected us."[1] Since the Annex protectors had been discovered on the premises, the Nazi officer arrested Victor Kugler and Johannes Kleiman. Bep Voskuijl evaded capture, and wandered the city in shock. Miep Gies, who refused to leave the offices, was questioned but not arrested. Miep spoke to the Nazi officer in German, and detected that he had the same Viennese accent she had as a child. When the officer realized Miep was Viennese, he screamed at her for hiding Jews, but did not take her into custody.

The eight residents from the Annex were transferred to a facility on the Weteringschans, which Eva Geiringer called a "proper regular prison for real criminals. Everyone ended up in these huge rooms where there were rows of bunks . . . The noise through the night of people crying and shouting, babies wailing—after being in hiding—it was like a madhouse. Terrible."[2]

Otto Frank found himself seated next to Johannes Kleiman. He whispered to Kleiman how terrible he felt that he and Kugler were arrested for sheltering his family. Kleiman replied: "Don't give it another thought. It was up to me, and I wouldn't have done it differently."[3]

Victor Kugler and Johannes Kleiman were transferred to an Amsterdam prison on Amstelveensweg for a month-long interrogation. SS Sergeant Karl Silberbauer, who had arrested them, was head interrogator. Kugler and Kleiman "had no idea whether they were going to live or be executed."[4]

Kleiman Is Freed from Jail

After his month's imprisonment Johannes Kleiman convinced the officials that he had bleeding stomach ulcers and would be useless in a forced labor prison. Amazingly, he was released for medical care and never recaptured. Miep and Bep saw him walking across the canal bridge. The women ran to him. Miep later wrote:

> We hugged each other hard. All three of us were laughing and crying at the same time . . . For a man who'd just been in a German prison camp, he looked better than I'd ever seen him . . . He laughed and said, 'The food at the camp was terrible. Just raw carrots, raw beets, sometimes watery soup. . . . For the first time in years, my ulcers are gone. All that raw food has cured my ulcers.[5]

Victor Kugler, however, was sent to Zwolle, Holland, where he endured forced labor until the winter of 1945.

Otto, Edith, Margot, and Anne stayed together, along with the Van Pels, as they were transported to Westerbork holding camp in Drente, Holland. Anne sat glued to the window during the train trip, drinking in the summer greenery. Otto later said:

> In our hearts . . . we were already anticipating the possibility that we might not remain in Westerbork to the end. . . . We also knew what was happening in Auschwitz, Treblinka . . . but then, were not the Russians already deep in Poland? The war was so far advanced that we could begin to place a little hope in luck.[6]

The Hard World of Westerbork

In Westerbork, Mrs. Rosa de Wieks recalled seeing Anne and Peter van Pels "always together. . . . Anne was lovely, . . . very pallid at first, but there was something so intensely attractive about her frailty and her expressive face . . . She was happy in Westerbork, though that seems almost incredible, for things were hard for us in the camp."[7]

Westerbork was barren and windy, described as being a sea of mud. Another girl, Janny Brandes-Brilleslijper, was put into the "S" barracks with the Frank women. These women were forced to break apart batteries and sort the tar and the carbon bars. She said: "we all began to cough because it gave off a certain kind of dust. The agreeable part . . . was that you could talk with each other . . . [and] exchange your thoughts."[8]

Another prisoner, Lenie de Jong, stated that the barracks was dirty, crammed with people, and infested. "Whatever you had, you put on the bunk bed and you kept your clothes on so the fleas wouldn't bother you quite so much."[9] Lenie de Jong's husband befriended Otto Frank, and Lenie got to know Edith, whom she said was always worrying about her girls. Mrs. De Wiek recalled that Edith was quiet, almost as if numbed, and each evening "she was always washing underclothing. The water was murky and there was no soap, but she went on washing, all the time."[10] Mrs. De Wiek claimed that her daughter and Anne were at least relieved to be out of hiding. They met new people, talked, even laughed.

Anne Grows Ill

Otto begged another prisoner, Rachel van Amerongen-Frankfoorder, to get Anne a job like hers, which was cleaning toilets and handing out uniforms to new arrivals. "Anne was very nice and also asked me if she could help me," Rachel said. She tried, but failed, to get this less taxing work for Anne.[11]

Soon Anne was taken ill. Family visits could be arranged, so Otto came to her bedside in the evening, and told her stories. As soon as Anne recovered, David, a twelve-year-old Orthodox Jewish boy who, because of his youth, lived in the women's barracks, got sick. When she was able, Anne stood by David's bed and comforted him. "He and Anne always talked about God," Mrs. De Wiek recalled, who marveled that Anne's faith had not failed her.[12]

The Cattle Car Journey to Hell

Paris was liberated on August 25, 1944, with a victory parade led by General Charles de Gaulle. Other French and Belgian cities were recovered by invading British, Canadian, and French armies. Yet, liberation would not come in time to free the inmates of Westerbork. On September 2, the Annex residents were packed along with over one thousand people onto the final train out of Westerbork to the east.

Anne, Peter, and their families clung together with sixty people crammed into a cattle car designed to hold eight cows. Otto urged everyone to be as courageous as possible. People had to sleep pressed against each other, and hover over the

111

few buckets used for toilets. Water was minimal and the stink grew unbearable.

Vera Laska, a Czech captive, recounted her horrifying cattle car experience:

> The woman next to me is dead . . . I have to stretch over her toward the slit in the window. . . . A bucketful of water is hurled in, cooling those at the middle . . . Most of the precious liquid drips down through the floorboards. It only intensifies the stench of human waste and vomit. Women cry, shriek, tear their hair.[13]

Another captive, Rose de Liema, described the cars opening after three torturous days and nights. "We stumbled out, and I had the feeling I had arrived in hell. It was night, chimneys were burning with huge bright flames. The SS beat everybody with sticks and guns."[14] This horrifying sight facing Anne was the concentration camp called Auschwitz.

The Selection Process Divides Families

As the cattle car riders who were still mobile thronged onto the platform, a loudspeaker roared: "Women to the left! Men to the right!" Anne and Margot clung to their mother as they saw Otto move off with Hermann and Peter van Pels, and Fritz Pfeffer. Ronnie Goldstein, a prisoner with the Frank women, said as she emerged into the lineup of women: "There stood Mengele, and he pointed—he didn't say anything: . . . To the right, that was us, the young, and in their eyes the healthiest people."[15]

The loudspeaker shouted: "It is an hour's march to the women's camp. For children and the sick there are trucks waiting at the end of the platform."[16] Anne had turned fifteen, so she was counted as a woman. All were given a quick examination by an SS doctor, which was often Dr. Josef Mengele. Ronnie Goldstein said she was put beside some

Hungarian women, and when they saw Mengele approach, one told her: "Here comes the angel of death."[17] If anyone appeared too ill to work, they got forced to the trucks. Anne, Edith, Margot, and Auguste van Pels passed. Not one of the old or sick women or children who went on the trucks was ever seen again. In most cases, they were taken directly to Auschwitz's gas chambers for execution.

Anne and the exhausted women were force-marched in the darkness to the section called Birkenau, a huge camp only for female prisoners.

A Humiliating Prison Initiation

Anne's thick brunette hair, so lovingly shampooed and styled during her years in hiding, was shaved off, along with her underarm and pubic hair. A cold gang shower with no soap or towels, plus a delousing liquid, finished this mortifying initiation into Birkenau. Each woman had been reduced to a dehumanized level. Anne received a worn sack-like dress and clogs. No coats, warm stockings, or underwear were distributed as a rule.

Anne Endures Filthy Beds, Inedible Food

As the fall weather turned wet and colder, the inmates of Birkenau started to suffer greatly. Another fifteen-year-old girl, Lilly Applebaum Lublin, joined Anne and Margot in the prison camp, after being in hiding for three years. Lilly later told of being "packed like sardines" in the three layers of bunk beds with vermin-infested straw mattresses. "If one person wanted to turn, we all had to turn, so we could move around."[18] Eventually the straw disintegrated, and women slept on bare boards with one blanket to wrap around them.

Lilly could barely stomach the food:

> A tin can of soup, which was so rotten and vile, when I tasted it, I couldn't eat it . . . I just ate the bread and drank a little water . . . Finally when I got so hungry . . . I said, "If I want to survive . . . I have to eat the soup." So I . . . remember forcing the soup down my throat, and big tears coming down my face. Eating and crying.[19]

Lilly questioned how this could be happening: "And here we are in Hell—human beings worse than animals. And nobody is doing anything about it . . . Where is the world?[20]

Roll Calls and Hard Labor Break Down Morale

Work gave some form to the endless days. Many women did useless jobs like digging up sod or stones. Roll call occurred before sunrise and again at night. This method of counting the prisoners forced the women to stand outdoors in perfect rows of fives, often for hours. Vera Laska said about the roll call: "Our shaven skulls blister in the scorching sun or are chilled by icy rains."[21]

Ronnie Goldstein stated that five women had to share one cup for water or the "so-called coffee . . . then five of you had to drink from that cup. Then we agreed, 'Remember, three sips for each person.' Anne Frank stood in the same group with me often, and we used the same little cup."[22] Everyone counted sips, because there would be no more liquid distributed and thirst became a torture. Anne became the leader of her circle of five, and also distributed the evening slices of bread, even though she was the youngest. This was because Anne was scrupulously fair.

Anne is Infected and Demoralized

Anne soon became infected with scabies. A special barracks was assigned to women with scabies, caused by mites burrowing into the skin and causing red, itching sores which are contagious. Janny Brandes-Brilleslijper told how they were inspected endlessly for this disease. "Everyone, . . . naked, out of the barracks. Mengele looked you over, from head to foot, and if you had pimples or a rash, then you could count on going to that side."[23] Mortified, Anne was diagnosed and sent to the scabies barracks. Margot asked to stay by Anne's side, and soon was infected herself.

Historians estimated that "the average life expectancy of a Jew who was not gassed on arrival was between six and seven weeks in Auschwitz."[24] Anne and Margot spent almost seven weeks in camp under abysmal conditions. When most had become hardened to the agony endured by others, Anne never lost her compassion. Mrs. De Wiek stood by Anne as they saw a group of naked Gypsy girls marching to the crematory, and marveled how Anne wept for them.[25]

Another selection was made at the end of October. Women were stripped naked, marched in front of a glaring searchlight, and selected for removal or death. Anne and Margot walked forward, heads up, bravely staring at Dr. Mengele as he selected them for removal.[26] Edith Frank, who had been smuggling bits of precious bread to them, was forced to watch Anne and Margot get taken from her. She was pulled away, screaming for her children. Trains left for Bergen-Belsen, near Hamburg in northern Germany, carrying Anne and Margot, and probably Gusti van Pels, along with about eight thousand Jewish women who still had the potential to work. Edith never left Birkenau, where she grew weaker from exhaustion, disease, and despair.

The Girls Land in Bergen-Belsen

By 1943, Bergen-Belsen was used for about ten thousand Jews who might be important enough to be exchanged for

Dr. Josef Mengele

A German physician, born in 1911, Josef Mengele's specialty was research into hereditary biology and genetics. Mengele joined the SS in 1938 and served in the medical corps on the Russian front. He then volunteered for Auschwitz and "became the chief medical officer of the camp on May 24, 1943."[27] Mengele realized he now had freedom to perform experiments at will upon a helpless population. According to the C.A.N.D.L.E.S. Holocaust Museum, "Twins provided the perfect experimental specimens. One could serve as a control while the other endured the experiments."[28] Historians explain that his job was to maintain the camp population balance by dividing all incoming Jews into two lines. The first provided laborers and possible subjects for his experiments, the second went straight to execution. Mengele also experimented on humans to help other Nazis design better equipment for soldiers.

The extent of Mengele's two years of inhumane experimentation is estimated through testimony of survivors. His Auschwitz records were destroyed before the Allies could get them. After the German surrender, Allied officials realized how many had died at Mengele's direction, including Hermann van Pels and Fritz Pfeffer. Mengele escaped to South America, and lived for thirty-five years under aliases, until he died by drowning in Brazil in 1979.

Germans imprisoned in other countries. As Anne and Margot arrived in November 1944, this camp was becoming a dumping ground for those who had overflowed the capacity of the gas chambers in other concentration camps.[29] There were no crematoriums at Bergen-Belsen.

Weak, hungry, freezing, and for the first time without a parent, Anne and Margot were forced to march four miles. They were then shoved into large tents that served as "temporary quarters for women from other concentration camps . . . several hundred women were crowded into . . . and left to cower on the damp clay soil."[30] During a storm, their tent was blown down.

Hannah Levy, a Jew from Serbia, kept a journal of these atrocious conditions. Hannah wrote: "November 8, 1944: . . . Our existence is cruel, animal like. All that is human in us, has been reduced to zero. . . . The damage to the soul goes so deep that your whole being seems to have withered away."[31] Daily food dwindled to a cup of soup of gray turnips normally fed to cattle. People were reduced to animalistic behaviors, such as fighting for scraps, to survive.

Anne Meets People She Loved

Hanne Goslar was staying alive at Bergen-Belsen through sheer determination that her sister Gabi would not be left without her. Incarcerated since June, Hanne reported the conditions after the storm blew down the tents. "Our beds, which were stacked in two levels, one above the other, were taken away, and we got stacks of three beds [to accommodate more prisoners per barracks]. . . . All people from the tents were taken to the barracks on the other side."[32]

Nanette Blitz, Anne's classmate from the Jewish Lyceum, told historian Melissa Muller that she chanced to meet her: Nanny "horrified at Anne's physical condition, her bald head, her sunken cheeks, her inflamed skin—told Anne about the fates of some of their friends, . . . for example, how Jacque van Maarsen had been saved by acquiring an 'Aryan' ID card."[33] Anne told Nanny that she hoped to survive the war, when she would write a book based on her diary. The greatest fear was that her parents had been executed. What Anne did not know was that the gas chambers were shut down on December 1, 1944. Auschwitz was being emptied, and Otto and Edith Frank were ill and emaciated, but alive.

Sisters Share a Celebration

The Frank sisters shared their barracks with the Daniels sisters and the Brilleslijper sisters, Lientje ("Lin") and Janny. The three pairs of sisters made a brave attempt to celebrate St. Nicholas Day, Chanukah, and Christmas: Janny bartered for some potato peelings, Anne found cloves of garlic, and the Daniels sisters rounded up a beet and a carrot. Lin sang for the barracks matrons and got some sauerkraut as a reward. "We saved a bit of bread from the rations, and each of us prepared a little surprise for the others . . ." As they shared this tiny feast, Anne described how they would order delicious foods from the best restaurant in Amsterdam, once they got home.[34]

Hanne Gives Anne All She Can

During February 1945, someone else who cared for Anne found her: Gusti van Pels. Gusti heard Hanne Goslar calling out for Dutch people. Realizing she was Anne's friend, she got them together for a meeting.

Hanne described their meeting: "The fence and the straw [barriers] were between us. . . . Maybe I saw her shadow. . . . She was a broken girl. I probably was, too. . . . She immediately began to cry, and she told me, 'I don't have any parents

Sick and dying survivors of Bergen-Belsen huddle under blankets after liberation in April 1945.

anymore.'" Anne told Hanne: "We don't have anything at all to eat here, . . . and we are cold; we don't have any clothes."[35] Hanne felt terrible, for at least in her block they kept their clothes. They met several more times, when Hanne was able to toss over a small Red Cross package of crackers and cookies, plus a few socks. This package was stolen away from Anne. Hanne tossed another package days later. This loving sacrifice kept Anne going.

Lin and Janny Brilleslijper smuggled bits of food to help Anne care for Margot. Both girls were ill with typhus, an acute infectious disease, where the bacteria causing it are borne by lice and fleas. If not treated, typhus causes severe stomach inflammation, high fever, skin eruptions, mental depression, and in its final stages, nervous system and brain damage. Janny, a nurse, spoke of her struggle to help the girls. She tried to keep Anne alive during the advanced stage of typhus, after she had fevered hallucinations:

> Anne stood in front of me, wrapped in a blanket . . . she had such a horror of the lice and fleas in her clothes that she had thrown all her clothes away. It was the middle of winter and she was wrapped in one blanket. I gathered everything I could find to give her so she was dressed again . . . I gave Anne some of our bread ration.[36]

Soon after that, the Frank sisters were gone from the barracks. They were found in the quarantine barracks the following day. Margot was barely conscious. "Margot's going to sleep well," Anne said. "And when she sleeps, I won't need to get up anymore . . . oh I'm so nice and warm."[37] Shortly after, Margot fell from her bunk to the floor, and died. Eva Geiringer said later, "When Margot died, Anne already believed that her mother and father were dead. And so she gave up."[38]

A few days later, the plankbed was empty. Lin and Janny found Anne's corpse, along with Margot's body. In her memoir, Lin wrote: "Four of us laid the thin bodies on a blanket and carried them to the great open grave. We could do no more."[39]

10

A Celebrated Writer

On April 15, 1945, less than a month after the death of Anne and Margot Frank, British troops arrived at Bergen-Belsen. The few thousand prisoners still able to walk had been made to drag the decomposing bodies of the dead and drop them into mass graves. Hiding these corpses could not be accomplished in time to fool the British. They forced the SS guards to finish the burials with bulldozers and disinfectants, trying to stop the spread of typhus and dysentery beyond the camp. Dysentery is a virulent bacterial disease, spread through foul water or contact with feces. When a prisoner contracted dysentery, the diarrhea from the disease, along with lack of drinking water, dehydrated the victim to the point of death.

No Jewish funeral services had been held for Anne Frank or any of the courageous inmates who perished. Anne, a girl who prayed daily, died alone with God at her side. Rabbis said prayers over the mass graves after liberation. The British soldiers rounded up the residents of the villages surrounding Bergen-Belsen, and made them march through every barracks. Colonel Spottiswoode forced them to look at the immense graves and pitiful survivors. He then said: "What you will see here is the final and utter condemnation of the Nazi Party. It justifies every measure which the United Nations will take to exterminate that Party."[1] Survivors and liberators joined in burning Bergen-Belsen to ashes, burying forever the grave of Anne Frank.

The Fate of Hidden Children

That the short, simple life of a Jewish schoolgirl from Amsterdam would endure in the hearts of millions seems inconceivable. Yet Anne Frank was destined to become the symbol of every child who was hidden, and every child who was lost in the Holocaust.

In 1939, when the war began, Anne and Margot Frank and Peter van Pels were just three of the approximately 1.6 million Jewish children living in territories to be occupied by the Nazis. According to research reported by the U.S. Holocaust Memorial Museum, between 1 to 1.5 million of those Jewish children were dead by May 1945.

Most of the European Jewish children who survived, did so because they remained hidden and undetected. The researchers of the "Life in the Shadows" exhibition at the U.S. Holocaust Memorial Museum stated: "these youngsters faced constant fear, dilemmas, and danger . . . a careless remark, a denunciation, or murmurings of inquisitive neighbors could lead to discovery and death."[2]

Many children were supported in hiding by underground groups or by gentiles who risked their own freedom to do what they thought was right. Hundreds of stories exist about children who were moved up to thirty times, who were enfolded into foster families and passed as members, or who along with a parent, had to hide in cramped, miserable cellars or attics. Children who were hidden in convent schools needed false Catholic identities created for them. Many of these children lost their Jewish identities. Unlike Anne, Margot, and Peter, most children hid separated from their natural parents, who were ultimately killed.

Hello Silberberg, Anne's boyfriend who was living in Amsterdam with grandparents, escaped Nazi captors and fled to his parents in Brussels. In an interview, Silberberg recalled that his family was "hidden by a lady on the outskirts of Brussels . . . We went into hiding in August '42 and we were liberated by the unit of the British Army on September 3, 1944 . . . the day the last transport left from Westerbork to Auschwitz with Anne Frank and her family."[3] Silberberg endured an arduous hiding experience, but was never betrayed like Anne Frank was.

The Netherlands had 3,372 rescuers, more than any other country. Through the determination of these 3,372 heroes, many Dutch Jewish children were saved. Unfortunately, of the twenty-five thousand Jews hidden in the Netherlands, only one-third to one-half lived to see the end of the war.[4] Two examples of the many children who were placed by the Dutch underground are Salomon and Eva Harrington, affectionately cared for by Johannes and Janke DeVries from 1942–1944, along with their own two children, in the southern Netherlands. DeVries said: "we always had to be careful. The Dutch Nazis were the worst because it was hard to know who they were. I saw one little girl being taken from the home where she was hiding, and I vowed never to let my kids be taken."[5] Salomon and Eva were reunited with their natural mother after the war.

Otto's Long Journey Home

Otto wrote in a letter after the war about his decline at Auschwitz, where he was severely depressed, starving, extremely weak and wracked with diarrhea, probably from dysentery.[6] Doctors at the sick barracks kept him alive. In January 1945, with Soviet troops fast advancing through Poland, the Nazi officers decided all prisoners well enough to walk would be made to march to another camp. Auschwitz camp prisoners were forced to leave, except for the men in the sick barracks.

On the night before the forced departure, Peter van Pels visited Otto, whom he had been seeing each evening. Otto said, "Peter acted like a son to help me. Every day he brought me extra food. . . . He never could stay long . . . and he never spoke about Anne."[7] Otto begged Peter to hide in the hospital and depend on the soldiers from the Soviet Union to liberate him. Peter said he was still strong, and his chance to survive was better if he made the march. If he was caught hiding, the Nazis would execute him. Otto wept to see him go.

In January 1945, Soviet troops defeated the remaining SS guards, and turned all of Auschwitz into a hospital. Although they had no real medications, Otto recalled that the freed prisoners were scrubbed, and given rations and clean clothes from the SS stores. The women survivors came up from Birkenau, among them Eva Geiringer. Although they had no news about each other's family members, Otto and Eva gave each other encouragement. By mid February, Otto and the Geiringers were removed from Auschwitz. Once released in Poland, Otto wrote of his liberation to his mother, sister, and family: "Where Edith and the children are, I do not know. We have been apart since 5 September 1944. I merely heard that they had been transported to Germany. One has to be hopeful, to see them back well and healthy."[8]

Rosa "Rootje" de Winter (called Rosa De Weik by Ernst Schnabel) was with Edith Frank to the end. After a short while in sick barracks, Edith died on January 6, 1945. Mrs. De Winter survived and encountered Otto where they were housed in Katowice, Poland. When she broke the news of Edith's death, Otto felt the loss of his wife deeply. He wrote to his mother: "Because Edith's news from January 6, which I now have, affects me so badly that I am not quite all with it. . ."[9]

With the help of the Soviet troops, Otto began his journey home to Amsterdam. While on a train, he was reunited with Eva Geiringer, who took him to her mother.[10] It appeared Erich and Heinz Geiringer perished at Auschwitz, along with Edith.

The War Ends Bitterly for All

The Allied forces decimated Germany and Austria throughout April 1945. On April 28, 1945, Benito Mussolini and other leaders of his fascist government in Italy were caught and assassinated as they tried to escape to Switzerland. In his bunker hideout beneath Berlin, Adolf Hitler committed suicide on April 30, 1945. Allied troops continued to fight for and aid the Netherlands, dropping food packages by air to the starving Dutch. On May 4, 1945, Admiral Doenitz, Hitler's appointed successor, informed General Montgomery that he would surrender German forces in the Netherlands, Denmark, and northern Germany. Although the war with Japan continued, the war with the Third Reich came to an end on May 7, 1945, when General Dwight Eisenhower and other Allied officers accepted unconditional German surrender.[11]

Otto wrote in his journal that on June 3, after nearly four months in transit, he arrived in Amsterdam. There he discovered that Kugler, Kleiman, and Lotte Kaletta, Fritz Pfeffer's beloved, had survived. Miep and Jan Gies offered Otto a home without a moment's hesitation. "You stay right here with us. You have a room here with us . . . for as long as you want," Miep said.[12] Although the Dutch had endured privations during 1944–1945 and had little themselves, these friends gave straight from their hearts.

Who Betrayed the Annex Residents?

Otto Frank never publicly discussed the matter of the betrayer. Miep Gies said in her 1987 book that the Dutch police investigated the betrayal in 1948, and found that someone had collected the bounty reward. No name was recorded. In 1963, a renewed investigation took place due to the enormous fame of the book, play, and movie versions of Anne's diary. Miep and Jan Gies claimed they still had no sure knowledge of the betrayer. SS Officer Karl Silberbauer who arrested the Annex residents, was asked if he recalled who was the betrayer. He said he did not.

Historian Carol Ann Lee interviewed individuals involved in this investigation, and read many documents. She stated in her 2002 book that the first suspect was Wilhelm van Maaren, hired as head warehouseman to take over for Johan Voskuijl. Van Maaren, although suspicious about hidden Jews, would probably not get involved with the police, because he was hiding his own eldest son from forced labor. Johannes Kleiman discovered through his accountant that a Dr. Bangert said he had a patient who knew about hidden Jews at 263 Prinsengracht a year before they were betrayed. He would not name the patient, but it was not Van Maaren.

Historian Melissa Muller stated she suspected the Hartogs. Lena cleaned the offices and Lammert worked as Van Maaren's warehouse assistant. During the first investigation,

Kleiman told the police that Lammert Hartog had disappeared abruptly when the police came to arrest the hidden Jews. This could have been because Hartog himself was avoiding his summons for forced labor in Germany. Muller also accused Lena Hartog as the betrayer, perhaps to get rid of any suspicion that her husband was involved in hiding Jews. However, in November 2000, Miep and her close friend Father John Neiman spoke about Muller's theory. Father Nieman stated that Miep said Lena was *not* the betrayer, but did not say how she knew.[13]

Carol Ann Lee points to a man named Tonny Ahlers. She suspects Ahlers was behind the burglary of sugar and ration books from the 263 Prinsengracht warehouses, a product he needed badly for his own Wehrmacht contracts. An active Nazi supporter, Ahlers had turned in others and openly hated Jews. Lee claims the bounty payment on eight Jews could have been as high as 320 guilders, enough to help save his failing business.[14] The tip to raid the Annex on August 4, 1944, came in to Julius Dettman at SD headquarters. Dettman committed suicide on July 25, 1945, before he could be questioned. Gestapo chief Willi Lages, interrogated in 1964, said he knew that the tip came from someone known to the SD, whose past information had been good. Years later, Tonny Ahler's brother stated that "Tonny told me he did it. . . . He was proud of it. He did it for the money."[15]

Otto's Final Loss

In July 1945, Otto reportedly found his daughters' names on the Red Cross lists of concentration camp dead. Anne and Margot were gone. He was told that their deaths were confirmed by Janny and Lin Brandes-Brilleslijper. Otto went to Lin's home in Laren to hear it from her own lips. He also found Janny for her testimony. "I had to tell him . . . that his children were no more," said Janny. "He took it very hard."[16] Jacqueline van Maarsen told of Otto's visits to her. "He cried and cried," Jacque said. "He came to see me often, and I was at a loss as to how to console him. The only thing I could do was talk to him about his children." Otto also spoke with Jetteke and Trees, two survivors who had been friends of Margot's. "Both of his daughters had been equally dear to him," Jacque said.[17]

Otto learned that Fritz Pfeffer had died in Neuengamme concentration camp in December 1944 of a disease of the intestines. Gusti van Pels was transported to Theresienstadt, and perished sometime in April. The site of her death has never been substantiated. Peter van Pels made the torturous march all the way to Mauthausen, where he "toiled in the camp's rock quarries. . . . He died [of disease and exhaustion] on May 5, 1945, the day the camp was liberated."[18] Later statistics proved that of the sixty-six thousand evacuated from the Auschwitz camps, about fifteen thousand died on marches.[19]

Miep Produces Anne's Legacy

Miep and Jan Gies kept Anne's diary and journals locked away, dreaming that Anne would return and they could place these pages in her hands. When Otto told Miep about Anne's death, she handed him the papers and the checkered diary she had saved and said: "Here is your daughter Anne's legacy to you."[20] Otto was overwhelmed with the record of Anne's life in hiding. He read it over and over, translating poignant sections into German, so his elderly mother could read them in Basel, Switzerland. When he asked Miep to read these sections, she found it too painful to do so.

Otto typed Anne's writings. According to editor Gerrold van der Stroom, he "only copied 'the essentials'. . . . He omitted whatever he felt would prove of no interest [to family] together with passages that might offend living persons, or remarks about Anne's mother that 'didn't concern anyone else.'"[21] Otto typed another copy based on Anne's loose sheets, which contained her edited second version of the diary entries up to March 29, 1944. He also typed selections from Anne's album and writing exercise books, still in their unedited version.

Otto handed Typescript I to his friend Albert Cauvern, a dramatist working for the Worker's Broadcasting Channel in Amsterdam. Cauvern improved the punctuation, spelling, word order, and used proper Dutch. He changed peoples' names as Anne had intended: the Van Pels family became the Van Daans, and Fritz Pfeffer became Albert Dussel. This revised manuscript became known as Typescript II. Otto expressed to his mother his determination to treasure every positive memory of Anne and Margot.

Anne's Diary Makes Publishing History

Since Anne had expressed her wish to publish the diary, Otto decided to do it for her. Various publishers turned the manuscript down, finding it too personal, intimate, and surprising in its sexual frankness for this period. By April 1946, a writer named Jan Romein read the diary and "was so deeply impressed that he wrote an article about it . . . in *Het Parool*."[22]

Readers of this Dutch publication were touched by Jan Romein's article entitled *Kinderstem* (A Child's Voice). Romein wrote that the Netherlands State Institute for War Documentation had already collected about two hundred diaries and journals detailing Dutch experiences. None, he thought, could be as 'pure, as intelligent and yet as human as this one.'"[23]

Romein stated:

> To me the fate of this Jewish girl epitomizes the worst
> crime perpetrated by everlastingly abominable minds.
> . . . this girl would have become a talented writer had
> she remained alive. . . . [She] showed an insight into the
> failings of human nature—her own not excepted—so
> infallible that it would have astonished one in an adult,
> let alone in a child.[24]

Publishers contracted to put out a Dutch edition of
Anne Frank's diary. Certain editorial changes, polishing,
and shortening occurred to Typescript II by the editors. At
last, in the summer of 1947, when Anne would have been
eighteen, her legacy was available for the Dutch public.
Otto used Anne's own title: *Het Achterhuis* [The Back
House, or Rear Annex]. Resulting from the popularity of the
diary in The Netherlands, German and French translations
were then published.

The English version of Anne's diary came out with
Doubleday and Company in Great Britain in May 1952 and in
the United States in June 1952, titled *Anne Frank: The Diary
of a Young Girl*. Otto was astonished at the huge reception,
large sales, and the immediate interest in stage and screen
rights. From 1950–1952, Otto grew closer to Elfriede
Geiringer. When her daughter Eva married Israeli financial
broker Zvi Schloss and settled with him in London, Otto
attended her wedding. Otto rediscovered love with "Fritzi,"
or "Sugarli," as he called her. They married in November
1953 at Amsterdam's City Hall, where the only guests were
Miep and Jan Gies and Johannes Kleiman and his wife.[25] The
couple went to live in Basel, Switzerland near Otto's relatives.

The play *The Diary of Anne Frank* premiered on Broadway
on October 5, 1955, to great success. Otto wrote to the cast
that it was impossible for him to actually see the play,

although he hoped that "the message which it contains will, through you, reach as many people as possible and awaken in them a sense of responsibility to humanity."[26] The play debuted in Amsterdam in November 1956, where Queen Juliana held an opening ceremony honoring Otto, the Gieses, Bep, and the Kleimans. Kugler by then lived in Canada. Before the curtain rose, Otto excused himself. The others experienced the joy and pain of seeing their own youthful selves live again on stage.

The Anne Frank House is Born

In 1956, the dilapidated building at 263 Prinsengracht was saved by the Amsterdam City Council so it could become a museum. It was presented the following year to the *Anne Frank Stichting*, the foundation started by a group of Amsterdam citizens. The building, today called The Anne Frank House, is used as an educational place for visitors to learn about the Holocaust and Anne Frank's beliefs and ideals. It opened to the public in 1960. As of 1999, a new exhibition building adjoined it. The staff reports that in 2000 "after the Rijkmuseum and the Van Gogh Museum, it is the most visited site in Amsterdam."[27] The original furnishings in the Annex were stripped by the Nazis, so the rooms remain empty. Anne's celebrity photos still decorate the dull, faded walls of her small bedroom.

Visitors write messages in the guest books. This example, by a Japanese girl, shows how Anne's legacy lives on:

> I am a fifteen year old girl and I was greatly impressed by the diary of Anne Frank. I have learned more from it than I ever learned in school. I have learned the following things: 1. We must not have war. 2. We must never lie. 3. We must not lose hope.[28]

The Cast of *The Diary of Anne Frank*, performed January 22, 1960, at Belleville Township High School, in Belleville, Illinois.

"When I was cast as Mrs. Van Daan (above, second from left) in our high school production of *The Diary of Anne Frank*, the details of the Holocaust were not taught in history class. As we rehearsed *The Diary*, I heard Anne's voice speaking through her entries. I saw the desperation grow within the three teens as they endured their years in hiding. This shook me to the core. Here are some memories, forty-five years later, of several members of that cast:

Out of an all-Christian cast, one actor had an understanding of what the Jews were facing. Lance Foster [Mr. Van Daan] had some Jewish heritage, and knew that 'quite a few of our relatives were left behind, mostly in Poland,' where many died. Lewis Bosworth [Dr. Dussel] connected with his character when he began wearing 'the yellow Star of David patch.' Sarajo Dunck Clifton [Margot] recalled how depressed she got during rehearsal, because 'they lived in darkness, it was never brightly lit . . . and you could never leave.' David Rasche [Peter] and I both remembered a sense of panic every time we made a noise. 'I'd never felt that kind of fear,' Rasche said. Clifton agreed: 'the fear was like a vice inside us, a tightness, that they were coming . . . the Nazis.' I still fight back tears when I recall from the play the Nazi police pounding on that door."[29]—Spring Hermann, author of this biography.

Institutions Carry On Anne's Legacy

The Anne Frank Zentrum in Berlin, Germany, coordinates a large international traveling exhibit called "Anne Frank— a History for Today" and moves people to become involved in current issues concerning discrimination and persecution. The Anne Frank Center in New York City has been working since 1977 to distribute exhibits in the United States, sent from the Anne Frank House in Amsterdam. Each June 12, they celebrate Anne's birthday and present the *Spirit of Anne Frank Award* to those helping to overcome racism and discrimination. In London, England, the Anne Frank Educational Trust UK, founded in 1991, also works with the Anne Frank House in teaching young people to reject discrimination. In Frankfurt, Germany, the Anne Frank Youth Center is located in the neighborhood of Alice Frank's (Otto's mother) former home. Anne's diary is commonly read in German schools, so students continue their dialogue about persecution in the past and today.

The name "Anne Frank" has been given to schools, homes for children and young people, and even to a hybrid rose and a tulip. Knowing how much Anne loved nature and spent her two years in hiding gazing at one chestnut tree, perhaps the most perfect tribute to her legacy is the Anne Frank Forest, a special planting of 10,000 trees in the Forest of the Martyrs, Judea, Israel.[30] In countless ways around the world, Anne's spirit lives eternally.

TIMELINE

(Shaded areas indicate events in the life of Anne Frank.)

1925
Otto Frank marries Edith Hollander.

1926
February 16: Margot is born in Frankfurt, Germany.

1929
June 12: Anne is born in Frankfurt, Germany.

October: New York stock market crash.

1933
Anne kept out of Aryan pre-school.

Hitler becomes chancellor of Germany.
March 22: Concentration camp at Dachau opens.
April 26: Gestapo established.
May 10: Nazis burn banned books in public.

December: Franks leave Germany forever.

1934
Family settles in Amsterdam. Anne thrives in Montessori kindergarten.

August 2: Hitler names himself "Fuhrer," or leader, of Germany.

1935
May 31: Jews in Germany no longer allowed to serve in armed forces.
September 15: Anti-Jewish Nuremberg Laws are enacted; Jews are no longer considered citizens of Germany.

1936
Otto's business is slow; Anne and Margot act as household help to Edith.

Nazis boycott Jewish-owned businesses.
March 7: Nazis occupy Rhineland.
July: Sachsenhausen concentration camp opens.

1937
July 15: Buchenwald concentration camp opens.

1938

Anne happy in school; Otto takes a business partner, Hermann van Pels.

March: Mauthausen concentration camp opens.

March 13: Germany annexes Austria and applies all anti-Jewish laws there.

July 6: League of Nations holds conference on Jewish refugees at Evian, France, but no action is taken to help the refugees.

October 5: All Jewish passports must now be stamped with a red "J."

October 15: Nazi troops occupy the Sudentenland.

November 9-10: Kristallnacht, the Night of the Broken Glass; Jewish businesses and synagogues are destroyed and 30,000 Jews are sent to concentration camps.

1939

Otto moves the business with Van Pels.

March: Oma Hollander moves in with the Franks.

March 15: Germans occupy Czechoslovakia.

August 23: Germany and the Soviet Union sign a non-aggression pact.

September 1: Germany invades Poland, beginning World War II.

October 28: First Polish ghetto established in Piotrkow, Poland.

November 23: Jews in Poland are forced to wear an arm band or yellow star.

1940

Anne and Margot are pen pals with the Wagner sisters in Iowa.

April 9: Germans occupy Denmark and southern Norway.

May 7: Lodz Ghetto is established.

May 10: Germans invade Belgium and the Netherlands.

May 20: Auschwitz concentration camp is established.

June 22: France surrenders to Germany.

September 27: Germany, Italy, and Japan form the Axis powers.

November 16: Warsaw Ghetto is established.

1941

Anne and Margot must attend Jewish schools.

February: Anti-Jewish legislation begins in the Netherlands.

June 22: Germany invades the Soviet Union.

July: Miep marries Jan Gies.

October: Auschwitz II (Birkenau) death camp is established.

1942

British air raids hit Amsterdam.

Anne begins her diary.

January 20: Wannsee Conference takes place in Berlin where the "Final Solution" is outlined.

March 17: Killings begin at Belzec death camp.

April: Edith sews yellow stars on clothes.

May: Killings begin at Sobibor death camp.

July 5: Margot gets call-up.

July 6: Frank family goes into hiding.

July 22: Treblinka concentration camp is established.

Summer–Winter: Mass deportations to death camps begin.

1943

Anne lives in hiding with Margot, Peter, and five adults. In cramped tense quarters, Anne uses her writing to survive, passes puberty, studies hard, turns fourteen.

March: Liquidation of Krakow Ghetto begins.

April 19: Warsaw ghetto uprising.

Fall: Liquidation of Minsk, Vilna, and Riga ghettos.

1944

Anne has growth spurt, falls in love with Peter. Burglaries scare her.

March-May: Germany occupies Hungary and begins deporting Hungarian Jews.

July 14: Soviet forces liberate Majdanek death camp.

August 4: Police arrest Anne, family, helpers.

Late August: Franks are imprisoned at Westerbork.

September 2: Franks are moved to Auschwitz.

November 8: Anne and Margot are sent to Bergen-Belsen.

November 8: Death march of Jews from Budapest to Austria begins.

1945

Anne reunites with Gusti van Pels, Nanny Blitz, and Hanne Goslar.

January 17: Auschwitz inmates begin death march.

March 1945: Margot and Anne die from starvation and typhus.

April 6-10: Buchenwald inmates sent on death march.

April 30: Hitler commits suicide.

May 8: Germany surrenders.

1947

Anne's Diary is published in the Netherlands.

1952

Anne's Diary is published in United States and Great Britain.

Chapter Notes

Chapter 1. Anne Frank Enters a Changing World

1. Melissa Muller, *Anne Frank; The Biography,* translated by Rita and Robert Kimber (New York: Henry Holt and Company, 1998), p. 13.

2. Carol Ann Lee, *The Hidden Life of Otto Frank* (New York: William Morrow/HarperCollins, 2003), p. 30. Copyright © by Carol Ann Lee. Reprints by permission of HarperCollins Publishers, Inc.

3. *Anne Frank in the World: 1929–1945,* compiled by the Anne Frank House (New York: Alfred A. Knopf, 2004), p. 12.

4. Ibid. pp. 18–19.

5. Ruud van der Rol and Rian Verhoeven, *Anne Frank. Beyond the Diary—A Photographic Remembrance* (New York: Viking/ Penguin Group, 1993), pp. 8–9.

6. Eleanor L. Turk, *The History of Germany* (Westport, Connecticut: Greenwood Press, 1999), p. 101.

7. Van der Rol and Verhoeven, p 16.

8. Saul Friedlander, *Nazi Germany and the Jews,* Vol. 1 (New York: HarperCollins, 1997), p. 26.

9. Lorraine Glennon, Ed., *The 20th Century* (New York: Century Books, Inc., JG Press, Inc, 1999), p. 206.

10. Lee, p. 24.

11. David Barnouw and Gerrold van der Stroom, Eds., *The Diary of Anne Frank: The Critical Edition* (New York: Doubleday, 1989), p. 1. From *The Diary of Anne Frank: The Critical Edition* by Anne Frank, copyright © 1986 by Anne Frank-Fonds, Basle/Switzerland, for all texts of Anne Frank. English Translation copyright © 1989 by Doubleday, a Division of Random House Inc., and by Penguin Books Ltd. Used by permission of Doubleday, a division of Random House, Inc.

12. Lee, p. 16.

13. Muller, p. 27.

14. Lee, p. 30.

15. *Anne Frank in the World,* p. 20.

16. Amos Elon, *The Pity of It All: A History of Jews in Germany: 1743–1933* (New York: Henry Holt & Company, 2002), p. 159.

17. Lee, p. 16.

18. Ibid. p. 31.
19. Friedlander, p. 18.
20. Lee, p. 33.
21. Muller, p. 21.
22. Ibid., p. 27
23. Ibid., p. 25.
24. *Anne Frank in the World*, p. 20.
25. Van der Rol and Verhoeven, p. 11.
26. Lee, p. 35.
27. Muller, p. 34.
28. Lee, p. 36.

Chapter 2. From Frankfurt to Amsterdam

1. *Anne Frank in the World. 1929–1945*, compiled by the Anne Frank House (New York, Alfred A Knopf, 1985), pp. 16–17.

2. Ernst Schnabel, *Anne Frank: A Portrait in Courage* (New York: Harcourt Brace, 1958), p. 25.

3. Carol Ann Lee, *Roses from the Earth: The Biography of Anne Frank* (New York: Penguin Books, 1999), p. 19.

4. Ibid. p. 18.

5. Melissa Muller, *Anne Frank: The Biography*, translated by Rita and Robert Kimber (New York: Henry Holt and Company, 1998), p. 41.

6. "Adolf Hitler," *Jewish Virtual Library*, n.d., <http://www.jewish virtuallibrary.org/jsource/Holocaust/hitler.html> (October 6, 2004).

7. Ian Kershaw, *Hitler: 1889–1936 Hubris* (New York: W.W. Norton & Company, 1998) p. 12.

8. Adolf Hitler, *Mein Kampf*, translated by Ralph Manheim (Boston: Houghton Mifflin & Company, 1971), p. 18.

9. "Adolf Hitler."

10. Hitler, p. 329.

11. Muller, p. 42.

12. Lee, p. 22.

13. *The Holocaust Encyclopedia*, Walter Laquer, Ed., (New Haven: Yale University Press, 2001) p. 137.

14. Richard Rhodes, *Master of Death*, (New York: Alfred A. Knopf, 2002), p. 3.

15. Carol Ann Lee, *The Hidden Life of Otto Frank* (New York: William Morrow/HarperCollins, 2002), p. 38. Copyright © by Carol Ann Lee. Reprints by permission of HarperCollins Publishers, Inc.

16. Schnabel, p. 27.

17. Lee, *The Hidden Life of Otto Frank*, p. 39.

18. Ibid., p. 40.

19. Ibid., p. 44.

20. Muller, p. 60.

21. Ibid., p. 54.

22. Lee, *The Hidden Life of Otto Frank*, p. 29.

23. Ibid., p. 27.

24. Miep Gies with Alison Leslie Gold, *Anne Frank Remembered: The Story of the Woman Who Helped to Hide the Frank Family* (New York: Touchstone/Simon and Schuster, 1987), p. 27. Reprinted with the permission of Simon & Schuster Adult Publishing Group. Copyright © 1987 by Miep Gies and Alison Gold. All rights reserved.

25. Ibid., p. 32.

26. Ibid., p. 37.

27. Muller, p. 68.

28. Michael R. Marrus, *The Holocaust in History* (Brandeis University Press /University Press of New England, 1987), p. 27.

29. Joshua M. Greene and Shiva Kumar, Eds., *Witness: Voices from the Holocaust* (New York: Free Press, Simon and Schuster, 2000), p. 6.

30. *The Holocaust Encyclopedia*, p. 44.

31. Eleanor L. Turk, *The History of Germany* (Westport, Connecticut: Greenwood Press, 1999), pp. 123–124.

32. Lee, *The Hidden Life of Otto Frank*, p. 54.

33. Ibid., p. 55.

34. Marrus, p. 90.

Chapter 3. A Nazi Invasion

1. Carol Ann Lee, *The Hidden Life of Otto Frank* (New York: William Morrow/HarperCollins, 2002), p. 60. Copyright © by Carol Ann Lee. Reprints by permission of HarperCollins Publishers, Inc.

2. Melissa Muller, *Anne Frank: The Biography*, translated by Rita and Robert Kimber (New York: Henry Holt and Company, 1998), pp. 95–96.

3. Ibid., p. 97.

4. Ruud van der Rol and Rian Verhoeven, *Anne Frank. Beyond the Diary—A Photographic Remembrance* (New York: Viking/Penguin Group, 1993), p. 28.

5. Ruud van der Rol, "Behind the Picture . . . Anne's Tenth Birthday," *Anne Frank Magazine*, Amsterdam: The Anne Frank House, 1999, p. 56.

6. Lee, p. 61.

7. Hagen Schulze, *Germany: A New History* (Cambridge, Mass.: Harvard University Press, 1998), p. 265.

8. Bob Moore, *Refugees from Nazi Germany in the Netherlands 1933–1940* (Martinus Nijhoff Publishers, 1986), p. 18.

9. Ibid., pp. 32–33.

10. Miep Gies with Alison Leslie Gold, *Anne Frank Remembered: The Story of the Woman Who Helped to Hide the Frank Family* (New York: Touchstone/Simon and Schuster, 1987), p. 53. Reprinted with the permission of Simon & Schuster Adult Publishing Group. Copyright © 1987 by Miep Gies and Alison Gold. All rights reserved.

11. Carol Ann Lee, *Roses from the Earth: The Biography of Anne Frank* (New York: Penguin Books, 1999), p. 48.

12. Lee, *The Hidden Life of Otto Frank*, p. 57.

13. Susan Goldman Rubin, *Searching for Anne Frank: Letters from Amsterdam to Iowa*, (New York: Harry N. Abrams, Inc. Publishers, 2003), pp. 10–11.

14. Ibid., p. 11.

15. Ibid., p. 14.

16. Ibid.

17. Eva Schloss, with Evelyn Julia Kent, *Eva's Story: A Survivor's Tale by the Step-sister of Anne Frank* (New York: St. Martin's Press, 1988), p. 31.

18. Ibid.

19. Ibid. p. 32.

20. Lee, *The Hidden Life of Otto Frank*, pp. 62–63.

21. Sommerville, Donald, *World War II Day by Day* (Greenwich, Conn.: Dorset/Brompton Books Corporation, 1989), pp. 31–33.

22. Gies and Gold, p. 59.

23. Ibid., pp. 60–61.

24. Joan Bos, "Dutch Royal Genealogy from Count Johann V of Nassau to Queen Beatrix of the Netherlands," *Joan's Dutch Royal Genealogy*,

September 5, 2004, <www.xs4all.nl/~kvenjb/genealogy_nl/nassau/nassau_tekst.htm> (October 6, 2004).

25. Lee, *The Hidden Life of Otto Frank*, p. 66.

26. Muller, pp. 107–108.

27. Ibid., p. 112.

28. Ernst Schnabel, *Anne Frank: A Portrait in Courage* (New York: Harcourt Brace, 1958), pp. 54–55.

29. Ibid., p. 55.

30. Muller, p. 125.

31. Ibid., p. 126.

32. Gies and Gold, p. 69.

33. Ibid., p. 75.

Chapter 4. Amsterdam in the Nazis' Grasp

1. Carol Ann Lee, *The Hidden Life of Otto Frank* (New York: William Morrow/HarperCollins, 2002), p. 78. Copyright © by Carol Ann Lee. Reprints by permission of HarperCollins Publishers, Inc.

2. Miep Gies with Alison Leslie Gold, *Anne Frank Remembered: The Story of the Woman Who Helped to Hide the Frank Family* (New York: Touchstone/Simon and Schuster, 1987), p. 83. Reprinted with the permission of Simon & Schuster Adult Publishing Group. Copyright © 1987 by Miep Gies and Alison Gold. All rights reserved.

3. Lee, p. 78.

4. Ibid., p. 79.

5. Eleanor L. Turk, *The History of Germany* (Westport, Connecticut: Greenwood Press, 1999), p. 116.

6. Ibid.

7. Carol Ann Lee, *Roses from the Earth: The Biography of Anne Frank* (New York: Penguin Books, 1999), p. 75.

8. Ibid.

9. Deborah Dwork, *Children with a Star: Jewish Youth in Nazi Europe* (New Haven: Yale University Press, 1991), pp. 18–19.

10. Melissa Muller, *Anne Frank: The Biography*, translated by Rita and Robert Kimber (New York: Henry Holt and Company, 1998), p. 130.

11. Conversation between the author and Pieter Kohnstam, August 5, 2004.

12. Jacqueline van Maarsen, *My Friend Anne Frank* (New York: Vantage Press, 1996), p. 18.

13. Ibid., p. 19.

14. Lee, *Roses from the Earth*, pp. 76–77.

15. Hagen Schultze, *Germany: A New History* (Cambridge, Mass.: Harvard University Press, 1998), p. 258.

16. Muller, p. 133.

17. Michael R. Marrus, *The Holocaust in History* (University Press of New England/Brandeis University, 1987), p. 32.

18. Ibid.

19. Ibid., p. 42.

20. Lee, *The Hidden Life of Otto Frank*, p. 90.

21. Gies and Gold, p. 83.

22. Muller, pp. 134–135.

23. Ernst Schnabel, *Anne Frank: A Portrait in Courage* (New York: Harcourt Brace, 1958), p. 67.

24. Hannah Erendt, *Eichmann in Jerusalem. A Report on the Banality of Evil* (New York: Penguin Books/Viking Penguin, 1977), pp. 27–28.

25. Peter Z. Malkin and Harry Stein, *Eichmann in my Hands* (New York: Warner Books, Inc., 1990), p. 30.

26. Ibid., p. 46.

27. Ibid.

28. Michael Berenbaum, *A Promise to Remember* (New York: Bulfinch Press/AOL Time Warner Book Group, 2003), p. 14.

29. Ibid.

30. Ibid. p. 15.

31. Lee, *The Hidden Life of Otto Frank*, p. 92.

32. Lee, *Roses from the Earth*, p. 94.

33. Van Maarsen, *My Friend Anne Frank*, p. 24.

34. *Anne Frank in the World: 1929–1945*, compiled by the Anne Frank House (New York, Alfred A Knopf, 2001), p. 91.

35. Dwork, p. 24.

36. Ibid., p. 25.

37. Ibid.

38. Van Maarsen, p. 25.

39. Gies and Gold, p. 87.

Chapter 5. The Franks Go Into Hiding

1. Jacqueline van Maarsen, *My Friend Anne Frank* (New York: Vantage Press, 1996), p. 25.

2. Melissa Muller, *Anne Frank: The Biography*, translated by Rita and Robert Kimber (New York: Henry Holt and Company, 1998), p. 131.

3. Ernst Schnabel, *Anne Frank, A Portrait in Courage* (New York: Harcourt Brace and Company, 1958), p. 73.

4. Muller, p. 138.

5. Hedda Rosner Kopf, *Understanding Anne Frank's* The Diary of a Young Girl: *A Student Casebook to Issues, Sources, and Historical Documents* (Westport, Conn.: Greenwood Press, 1997), p. 97.

6. Michael R. Marrus, *The Holocaust in History*, University Press of New England, 1987, pp. 127–128.

7. Carol Ann Lee, *Roses from the Earth: The Biography of Anne Frank* (New York: Penguin Books, 1999), p. 98.

8. Ruud van der Rol and Rian Verhoeven, *Anne Frank. Beyond the Diary—A Photographic Remembrance* (New York: Viking/Penguin Group, 1993), p. 35.

9. Miep Gies with Alison Leslie Gold, *Anne Frank Remembered: The Story of the Woman Who Helped to Hide the Frank Family* (New York: Touchstone/Simon and Schuster, 1987), p. 87. Reprinted with the permission of Simon & Schuster Adult Publishing Group. Copyright © 1987 by Miep Gies and Alison Gold. All rights reserved.

10. Ibid., p. 88.

11. Hello Silberberg, Interview in "Anne Frank: The Life of a Young Girl," a film by Biography/A&E, 1979.

12. Van der Rol and Verhoeven, p. 38.

13. Gies and Gold, p. 29.

14. Ibid., p. 11.

15. Susan Goldman Rubin, *Searching for Anne Frank: Letters from Amsterdam to Iowa*, (New York: Harry N. Abrams, Inc. Publishers, 2003), p. 130.

16. David Barnouw and Gerrold Van der Stroom, Eds., *The Diary of Anne Frank: The Critical Edition* (New York: Doubleday, 1989), pp. 201. From *The Diary of Anne Frank: The Critical Edition* by Anne Frank, copyright © 1986 by Anne Frank-Fonds, Basle/Switzerland, for all texts of Anne Frank. English Translation copyright © 1989 by Doubleday, a Division

of Random House Inc., and by Penguin Books Ltd. Used by permission of Doubleday, a division of Random House, Inc.

17. Ibid., p. 202.

18. Ibid., pp. 206–207.

19. Eva Schloss with Evelyn Julia Kent, *Eva's Story: A Survivor's Tale by the Step-sister of Anne Frank* (New York: St. Martin's Press, 1988), pp. 38–39.

20. Gies and Gold, p. 94.

21. Ibid., pp. 94–95.

22. Ibid., p. 95.

23. Van Maarsen, p. 26.

24. Lee, p. 107.

25. Barnouw and Van der Stroom, p. 208.

26. Ibid. p. 209.

27. Hyman Aaron Enzer and Sandra Solotaroff Enzer, Eds., *Anne Frank: Reflections on her Life and Legacy*, Testimony of Hannah Pick-Goslar (Urbana, IL: University of Illinois Press, 2000), pp. 47–48.

28. Van Maarsen, p. 27.

29. Barnouw and Van der Stroom, p. 214.

30. Muller, p. 166.

31. Ibid., p. 167.

32. Barnouw and Van der Stroom, p. 216.

33. Ibid., p. 218.

34. Ibid., p. 226.

35. Ibid., p. 233.

Chapter 6. Life in the Annex

1. Miep Gies with Alison Leslie Gold, *Anne Frank Remembered: The Story of the Woman Who Helped to Hide the Frank Family* (New York: Touchstone/Simon and Schuster, 1987), p. 104. Reprinted with the permission of Simon & Schuster Adult Publishing Group. Copyright © 1987 by Miep Gies and Alison Gold. All rights reserved.

2. David Barnouw and Gerrold Van der Stroom, Eds., *The Diary of Anne Frank: The Critical Edition* (New York: Doubleday, 1989), p. 233. From *The Diary of Anne Frank: The Critical Edition* by Anne Frank, copyright © 1986 by Anne Frank-Fonds, Basle/Switzerland, for all texts of Anne Frank. English Translation copyright © 1989 by Doubleday, a

Division of Random House Inc., and by Penguin Books Ltd. Used by permission of Doubleday, a division of Random House, Inc.

3. Ibid. p. 234.

5. Ibid., p. 17.

4. Willy Lindwer, *The Last Seven Months of Anne Frank* (New York: Pantheon Books/Random House, 1991), p. 13.

6. Melissa Muller, *Anne Frank: The Biography*, translated by Rita and Robert Kimber (New York: Henry Holt and Company, 1998), p. 182.

7. Barnouw and Van der Stroom, p. 257.

8. Ibid.

9. Gies and Gold, p. 111.

10. Barnouw and Van der Stroom, p. 262.

11. Ibid., p. 263.

12. Ibid., p. 262.

13. Ibid., p. 266.

14. Carol Ann Lee, *The Hidden Life of Otto Frank* (New York: William Morrow/HarperCollins, 2002), p. 56. Copyright © by Carol Ann Lee. Reprints by permission of HarperCollins Publishers, Inc.

15. Ibid., p. 99.

16. Ruud van der Rol and Rian Verhoeven, *Anne Frank. Beyond the Diary—A Photographic Remembrance* (New York: Viking/Penguin Group, 1993), p. 63.

17. Barnouw and Van der Stroom, p. 321.

18. Muller, p. 191.

19. Ibid., p. 193.

20. Ibid.

21. Donald Sommerville, *World War II Day by Day*, (Greenwich, CT: Dorset Press, 1989), pp. 172–173.

22. Carol Ann Lee, *Roses from the Earth: The Biography of Anne Frank* (New York: Penguin Books, 1999), p. 122.

23. Barnouw and Van der Stroom, p. 352.

24. Ibid., p. 358.

25. Barnouw and Van der Stroom, pp. 361–362.

26. *Anne Frank's Tales from the Secret Annex* (Pocket Books/ Washington Square Press, 1983), p. 106.

27. Based on the author's observations of the original writings of Anne Frank displayed at the Anne Frank House, 263 Prinsengracht, Amsterdam, The Netherlands, May 2004.

28. Barnouw and Van der Stroom, p. 371.

29. Ibid. p. 374.

Chapter 7. The Young Writer

1. Carol Ann Lee, *The Hidden Life of Otto Frank* (New York: William Morrow/HarperCollins, 2002), p. 103. Copyright © by Carol Ann Lee. Reprints by permission of HarperCollins Publishers, Inc.

2. Ibid., pp. 103–104.

3. Ernst Schnabel, *Anne Frank, A Portrait in Courage* (New York: Harcourt Brace and Company, 1958), p. 92.

4. David Barnouw and Gerrold Van der Stroom, Eds., *The Diary of Anne Frank: The Critical Edition* (New York: Doubleday, 1989), p. 405. From *The Diary of Anne Frank: The Critical Edition* by Anne Frank, copyright © 1986 by Anne Frank-Fonds, Basle/Switzerland, for all texts of Anne Frank. English Translation copyright © 1989 by Doubleday, a Division of Random House Inc., and by Penguin Books Ltd. Used by permission of Doubleday, a division of Random House, Inc.

5. Curatorial brochure accompanying *"Anne Frank The Writer, An Unfinished Story,"* a joint project of the United States Holocaust Memorial Museum and the Netherlands Institute for War Documentation in association with the Anne Frank-Fonds with support from the Anne Frank House. USHMM, 2003.

6. *Anne Frank's Tales from the Secret Annex* (Pocket Books/ Washington Square Press, 1983), p. 13.

7. Barnouw and Van der Stroom, p. 409.

8. Ibid.

9. Ibid.

10. Ibid., p. 416.

11. Ibid., p. 422.

12. Hyman Aaron Enzer and Sandra Solotaroff Enzer, Editors, *Anne Frank: Reflections on her Life and Legacy*, Testimony of Hannah Pick-Goslar (Urbana, IL: University of Illinois Press, 2000), pp. 48–49.

13. Lorraine Glennon, Editor in Chief, *The 20th Century* (New York: JG Press, Inc./Century Books, Inc., 1999), p. 320.

14. Ibid., p. 321.

15. Donald Sommerville, *World War II Day by Day* (Greenwich, Conn.: Dorset Press, 1989), p. 207.

16. Miep Gies with Alison Leslie Gold, *Anne Frank Remembered: The Story of the Woman Who Helped to Hide the Frank Family* (New York: Touchstone/Simon and Schuster, 1987), p. 159. Reprinted with the permission of Simon & Schuster Adult Publishing Group. Copyright © 1987 by Miep Gies and Alison Gold. All rights reserved.

17. Ibid., p. 161.

18. Geoffrey Perret, *Eisenhower* (New York: Random House, 1999), p. 34.

19. Ibid., p. 100.

20. Stephen E. Ambrose, *Eisenhower: Volume One* (New York: Simon and Schuster, 1983), p. 122.

21. Ibid., p. 148.

22. Barnouw and Van der Stroom, p. 425.

23. Ibid., p. 428.

24. Gies and Gold, p. 170.

25. *Anne Frank's Tales from the Secret Annex*, p. 123.

26. Barnouw and Van der Stroom, pp. 431–432.

27. Ibid., p. 442.

28. Ibid., p. 482.

29. Melissa Muller, *Anne Frank: The Biography*, translated by Rita and Robert Kimber (New York: Henry Holt and Company, 1998), p. 215.

30. Gies and Gold, p. 174.

31. *Anne Frank's Tales from the Secret Annex*, p. 41.

32. Barnouw and Van der Stroom, p. 472.

33. Ibid. p. 550.

34. Ibid.

35. Ibid., p. 552.

36. Ruud van der Rol and Rian Verhoeven, *Anne Frank. Beyond the Diary—A Photographic Remembrance* (New York: Viking/Penguin Group, 1993), p. 73.

Chapter 8. A Threat Outside the Door

1. David Barnouw and Gerrold Van der Stroom, Eds., *The Diary of Anne Frank: The Critical Edition* (New York: Doubleday, 1989), p. 559.

From *The Diary of Anne Frank: The Critical Edition* by Anne Frank, copyright © 1986 by Anne Frank-Fonds, Basle/Switzerland, for all texts of Anne Frank. English Translation copyright © 1989 by Doubleday, a Division of Random House Inc., and by Penguin Books Ltd. Used by permission of Doubleday, a division of Random House, Inc.

2. Ibid., p. 569.

3. Ibid., p. 510.

4. Ibid., pp. 502–503.

5. Carol Ann Lee, *The Hidden Life of Otto Frank* (New York: William Morrow/HarperCollins, 2002), pp. 202–203. Copyright © by Carol Ann Lee. Reprints by permission of HarperCollins Publishers, Inc.

6. Curatorial booklet, *"Anne Frank the Writer. An Unfinished Story,"* Washington, D.C.: United States Holocaust Memorial Museum, 2003.

7. Barnouw and Van der Stroom, p. 578.

8. Ibid., p. 572.

9. Ibid., p. 582.

10. Michael R. Marrus, *The Holocaust in History* (University Press of New England, 1987), p. 184.

11. Barnouw and Van der Stroom, p. 585.

12. Miep Gies with Alison Leslie Gold, *Anne Frank Remembered: The Story of the Woman Who Helped to Hide the Frank Family* (New York: Touchstone/Simon and Schuster, 1987), p. 180. Reprinted with the permission of Simon & Schuster Adult Publishing Group. Copyright © 1987 by Miep Gies and Alison Gold. All rights reserved.

13. Ibid., p. 181.

14. Barnouw and Van der Stroom, p. 599.

15. Gies and Gold, p.182.

16. Barnouw and Van der Stroom, p. 609.

17. Vera Laska, Editor, *Women in the Resistance and in the Holocaust* (Westport, CT: Greenwood Press, 1983), p. 84.

18. Eva Schloss with Evelyn Julia Kent, *Eva's Story: A Survivor's Tale by the Step-sister of Anne Frank* (New York: St. Martin's Press, 1988), p. 89.

19. Ibid., p. 44.

20. Ibid., p. 45.

21. Ibid., p. 57.

22. Personal letter from Eva Geiringer Schloss, August 20, 2004.

23. Barnouw and Van der Stroom, p. 627.

24. Ibid., p. 628.

25. Ibid., p. 630.

26. Ibid., p. 648.

27. Ibid., pp. 656–667.

28. Donald Sommerville, *World War II Day by Day* (Greenwich, Conn.: Dorset Press, 1989), p. 231.

29. Gies and Gold, p. 183.

30. Melissa Muller, *Anne Frank: The Biography*, translated by Rita and Robert Kimber (New York: Henry Holt and Company, 1998), p. 226.

31. Barnouw and Van der Stroom, p. 672.

32. Ibid.

33. Ibid., p. 694.

34. Gies and Gold, p. 194.

35. Ernst Schnabel, *Anne Frank, A Portrait in Courage*, (New York: Harcourt Brace and Company, 1958), p. 135.

Chapter 9. Anne in Prison

1. Carol Ann Lee, *Roses from the Earth: The Biography of Anne Frank* (New York: Penguin Books, 1999), pp. 152–153.

2. Ibid.

3. Ernst Schnabel, *Anne Frank: A Portrait in Courage* (New York: Harcourt Brace and Company, 1958), p. 145.

4. Lee, p. 153.

5. Miep Gies with Alison Leslie Gold, *Anne Frank Remembered: The Story of the Woman Who Helped to Hide the Frank Family* (New York: Touchstone/Simon and Schuster, 1987), p. 210. Reprinted with the permission of Simon & Schuster Adult Publishing Group. Copyright © 1987 by Miep Gies and Alison Gold. All rights reserved.

6. Ernst Schnabel, *Anne Frank: A Portrait in Courage* (New York: Harcourt Brace and Company, 1958), p. 147.

7. Ibid., p. 158.

8. Willy Lindwer, *The Last Seven Months of Anne Frank* (New York: Pantheon Books/Random House, 1991) p. 52.

9. Ibid., p. 142.

10. Schnabel, p. 159.

11. Carol Ann Lee, *The Hidden Life of Otto Frank* (New York: William Morrow/HarperCollins, 2002), p. 135. Copyright © by Carol Ann Lee. Reprints by permission of HarperCollins Publishers, Inc.

12. Schnabel, p. 159.

13. Vera Laska, Ed., *Women in the Resistance and in the Holocaust: The Voices of Eyewitnesses* (Westport, Conn.: Greenwood Press, 1983), p. 175.

14. Lee, *The Hidden Life of Otto Frank*, p. 140.

15. Lindwer, p. 179.

16. Schnabel, p. 163.

17. Lindwer, p. 186.

18. Michael Berenbaum, *A Promise to Remember: The Holocaust in the Words and Voices of Its Survivors* (New York: Bulfinch Press/AOL Time Warner, 2003), p. 19.

19. Ibid., pp. 19–20.

20. Ibid., p. 20.

21. Laska, p. 178.

22. Lindwer, pp. 182–183.

23. Ibid., p. 62.

24. Lee, *The Hidden Life of Otto Frank*, p. 146.

25. Schnabel, pp. 168–169.

26. Lee, *Roses from the Earth*, p. 177.

27. "Josef Mengele," *Fact Index*, n.d., <http://www.fact-index.com/j/jo/josef_mengele> (October 6, 2004).

28. "Mengele," *C.A.N.D.L.E.S. Holocaust Museum*, n.d., <http://www.candles-museum.com/mengele.htm> (October 6, 2004).

29. Laska, p. 248.

30. Melissa Muller, *Anne Frank: The Biography*, translated by Rita and Robert Kimber (New York: Henry Holt and Company, 1998), pp. 252–253.

31. Laska, p. 254.

32. Lindwer, pp. 26–27.

33. Muller, p. 255.

34. Hyman Aaron Enzer and Sandra Solotaroff-Enzer, Eds., *Anne Frank: Reflections on her Life and Legacy*, Testimony of Hannah Pick-Goslar (Urbana, Ill.: University of Illinois Press, 2000), pp. 53–54.

35. Lindwer, p. 28.

36. Ibid., p. 74.

37. Carol Ann Lee, *Roses from the Earth*, p. 197.

38. Ibid.

39. Ibid., p. 198.

Chapter 10. A Celebrated Writer

1. Carol Ann Lee, *Roses from the Earth: The Biography of Anne Frank* (New York: Penguin Books, 1999), p. 199.

2. United States Holocaust Memorial Museum, "Life in the Shadows" exhibition booklet, 2004.

3. James Still, *And Then They Came for Me: Remembering the World of Anne Frank* (Woodstock, IL: Dramatic Publishing, 1999), p. 81.

4. Gay Block and Malka Drucker, *Rescuers: Portraits of Moral Courage in the Holocaust* (New York: Holmes & Meier Publishers, Inc.; TV Books L.L.C. revised edition, 1992), p. 45.

5. Ibid., p. 50.

6. Carol Ann Lee, *The Hidden Life of Otto Frank* (New York: William Morrow/HarperCollins, 2002), p. 150. Copyright © by Carol Ann Lee. Reprints by permission of HarperCollins Publishers, Inc.

7. Ibid., p. 152.

8. Ibid., p. 161.

9. Ibid., p. 166.

10. David Barnouw and Gerrold Van der Stroom, Eds., *The Diary of Anne Frank: The Critical Edition* (New York: Doubleday, 1989), p. 55. From *The Diary of Anne Frank: The Critical Edition* by Anne Frank, copyright © 1986 by Anne Frank-Fonds, Basle/Switzerland, for all texts of Anne Frank. English Translation copyright © 1989 by Doubleday, a Division of Random House Inc., and by Penguin Books Ltd. Used by permission of Doubleday, a division of Random House, Inc.

11. Donald Sommerville, *World War II Day by Day*, pp. 302–304.

12. Miep Gies with Alison Leslie Gold, *Anne Frank Remembered: The Story of the Woman Who Helped to Hide the Frank Family* (New York: Touchstone/Simon and Schuster, 1987), p. 231. Reprinted with the permission of Simon & Schuster Adult Publishing Group. Copyright © 1987 by Miep Gies and Alison Gold. All rights reserved.

13. Lee, *The Hidden Life of Otto Frank*, p. 123.

14. Ibid., p. 125.

15. Ibid., p. 129.

16. Willy Lindwer, *Last Seven Months of Anne Frank* (New York: Pantheon Books/Random House, 1991), p. 84.

17. Jacqueline van Maarsen, *My Friend Anne Frank* (New York: Vantage Press, 1996), pp. 52–53.

18. Lee, *The Hidden Life of Otto Frank*, p. 195.

19. *The Holocaust Encyclopedia*, Walter Laquer, Editor, (New Haven: Yale University Press, 2001) p. 137.

20. Gies and Gold, p. 235.

21. Barnouw and Van der Stroom, p. 62.

22. Ibid., p. 67.

23. Ruud van der Rol and Rian Verhoeven, *Anne Frank. Beyond the Diary—A Photographic Remembrance* (New York: Viking/Penguin Group, 1993), pp. 103, 105.

24. Barnouw and Van der Stroom, pp. 67–68.

25. Lee, *The Hidden Life of Otto Frank*, p. 249.

26. Ibid., p. 255.

27. James E. Young, "The Anne Frank House: An Accessible Window to the Holocaust," *Anne Frank Magazine*, 1999 Edition, p. 13.

28. Anne G. Steenmeijer, Editor, *A Tribute to Anne Frank*, (New York: Doubleday and Company, Inc., 1970), p. 84.

29. These remarks are taken from conversations between the author and Sarajo Dunck Clifton, Lance Foster, and David Rasche, and letters to the author from Lewis Bosworth and James Fischer, during August, 2004.

30. Ibid., p. 119.

Glossary

anti-Semitism—A negative belief which causes a person to deny equal rights and freedoms for Jews.

Aryan—According to the Nazis, a person with pure Nordic or Caucasian descendants and blood line.

black market—A term used for an illegal network of sellers of goods or changers of money violating officially controlled quotas, used commonly when countries are under occupation.

Chanukah—Anglicized spelling of the Jewish holiday Hanukkah (in Hebrew). This eight-day holiday celebrates the victory of the Hebrew group called the Maccabees over the Syrians, and the rededication of their temple in Jerusalem in 165 B.C.

curfew—A fixed time after which no members of an assigned group can be away from home. Curfews were fixed for Jews by the Nazi regime in all cities they controlled.

fascist—A person who follows a political ideology of the extreme conservative right. In Italy in 1922–1943, dictator Benito Mussolini coined the term from the Roman *fasces*, symbols of law and order. His fascist government used extreme force to maintain power.

Gestapo—*Geheime Stats Polizei* in German. This secret state police force was mainly responsible for political investigations and arrests.

ghetto—A quarter of a city where an ethnic minority, often Jews, were forced to reside. Many ghettos were walled with a locked gate.

gymnasium—The name given in Germany to a private secondary school.

Kristallnacht—The Night of Broken Glass, on November 9, 1938, in which Storm Troopers, rousing citizens to join them, destroyed Jewish businesses and synagogues throughout Germany.

Mein Kampf—Translated, "My Struggle," this lengthy political treatise—part autobiography, part philosophy—was written by Adolph Hitler in prison in 1924 to explain his plan to raise up the German "master race" and destroy the Jews.

National Socialist German Worker's Party [NSDAP]—A radical socialist party founded in 1919, and taken over in the early 1920s by Adolph Hitler and his supporters. It supposedly represented the average German worker on hard times after World War I and during the depression.

NAZI—These are initials derived from the German term NAtionalsoZIalistiche, the common name for the NSDAP.

quarantine—A place where persons with contagious diseases are isolated.

Reichstag—Name for the lower chamber of the German parliament from 1871–1945.

resistance—An organization of citizens working underground against armed forces occupying their country.

SD—*Sicherheitsdienst* in German. The intelligence or espionage branch of the SS, which reported directly to Nazi top officials.

SS—*Schutzstaffel* in German. The security police force that answered directly to Hitler and the Nazi top officials, outside of German law.

Storm Troopers—Called the SA, or in German, *Sturm abteilung*. These were men who joined a militia run by the Nazi party and wore dark brown uniforms, inspiring the nickname "Brown Shirts." Their job was to harass any group opposed to Nazi domination, particularly Jews, and run hate rallies.

Third Reich—The term Adolph Hitler gave to his Nazi government, which ruled from 1933–1945. Germans called the Holy Roman Empire (962–1806) the First Reich, and the German Empire (1871–1918) the Second Reich.

valerian—An herb long used to treat anxiety and depression.

Wehrmacht—The German term for the army of the Third Reich.

Weimar Republic—The first German parliamentary democratic government, established after Kaiser Wilhelm II abdicated. Its constitution was drawn up at the city of Weimar in August 1919, thus giving the republic its title. Due to severe economic crises, the Weimar Republic collapsed in 1930, and the government was taken over by the NSDAP.

Further Reading

Anne Frank's Own Writings:

Anne Frank's Tales from the Secret Annex. New York: Pocket Books/ Washington Square Press, 1983.

Barnouw, David and Gerrold Van der Stroom, Eds. *The Diary of Anne Frank: The Critical Edition.* New York: Doubleday, 1989.

Anne Frank's Life and Family:

The Anne Frank House. *Anne Frank in the World.* New York: Alfred A. Knopf, 2001.

Gies, Miep. *Anne Frank Remembered.* New York: Touchstone/ Simon and Schuster, 1987.

Lee, Carol Ann. *The Hidden Life of Otto Frank.* New York: William Morrow/HarperCollins, 2003.

_____. *Roses from the Earth: The Biography of Anne Frank.* New York: Penguin Books, 1999.

Muller, Melissa. *Anne Frank: The Biography*, translated by Rita and Robert Kimber. New York: Henry Holt and Company, 1998.

Rubin, Susan Goldman. *Searching for Anne Frank: Letters from Amsterdam to Iowa.* New York: Harry N. Abrams, Inc. Publishers, 2003.

van der Rol, Ruud and Rian Verhoeven. *Anne Frank. Beyond the Diary—A Photographic Remembrance.* New York: Viking/ Penguin Group, 1993.

van Maarsen, Jacqueline. *My Friend Anne Frank.* New York: Vantage Press, 1996.

Hiding, Enduring, and Surviving the Concentration Camps:

Bleier, Inge Joseph and David E. Gumpert. *Inge: A Girl's Journey Through Nazi Europe.* Grand Rapids, Mich.: William B. Eerdmans Publishing, 2004.

Block, Gay and Malka Drucker. *Rescuers: Portraits of Moral Courage in the Holocaust.* New York: Holmes & Meier Publishers, Inc. TV Books L.L.C. revised edition, 1992.

Brooks, Philip. *Viewing the Holocaust Today.* Chicago, Ill.: Heinemann Library, 2003.

Greenfield, Howard. *After the Holocaust.* New York: Greenwillow Books, 2001.

Holocaust Encyclopedia. Edited by Walter LaQuer. New Haven: Yale University Press, 2001.

Levy, Pat. *The Holocaust.* North Mankato, Minn.: Smart Apple Media, 2003.

Lindwer, Willy. *Last Seven Months of Anne Frank.* New York: Pantheon Books/Random House, 1991.

Schloss, Eva, with Evelyn Julia Kent. *Eva's Story: A Survivor's Tale by the Step-sister of Anne Frank.* New York: St. Martin's Press, 1988 (rep. Berkeley Books, 1990).

Willoughby, Susan. *Art, Music, and Writings From the Holocaust.* Chicago, Ill.: Heinmann Library, 2003.

Witness: Voices from the Holocaust. Edited by Joshua M. Greene and Shiva Kumar. New York: Free Press, Simon and Schuster, 2000.

Women in the Resistance and in the Holocaust. Vera Laska, Editor. Westport, CT: Greenwood Press, 1983.

The Holocaust

Bleier, Inge Joseph and David E. Gumpert. *Inge: A Girl's Journey Through Nazi Europe.* Grand Rapids, Mich.: William B. Eerdmans Publishing, 2004.

Brooks, Philip. *Viewing the Holocaust Today.* Chicago, Ill.: Heinemann Library, 2003.

Greenfield, Howard. *After the Holocaust.* New York: Greenwillow Books, 2001.

Levy, Pat. *The Holocaust.* North Mankato, Minn.: Smart Apple Media, 2003.

Willoughby, Susan. *Art, Music, and Writings From the Holocaust.* Chicago, Ill.: Heinmann Library, 2003.

Internet Addresses

The Anne Frank Center in New York, NY.
<http://www.annefrank.com>

The Anne Frank House in Amsterdam, Netherlands.
<http://www.annefrank.nl>

The Anne Frank Youth Center, Frankfurt am Main, Germany.
<http://www.jbs-anne-frank.de>

The Jewish Virtual Library, the source of many research articles on the Holocaust and its figures.
<http://www.us-israel.org>

Index